D1543344

Daisy Cakes

Introduction by Shark Tank's Barbara Corcoran

KIM DAISY

share a slice of love!

Lydia Inglett Ltd. Publishing

This book is lovingly dedicated
to my mother Geraldine Bishop Adams
and to cooks and bakers everywhere
who know that deep down
cooking for someone
really is an act of love.

Daisy Cakes, Share A Slice Of Love

by Kim Daisy

ISBN-13:978-1-938417-15-3

Copyright © 2014 Original content only

www.ilovedaisycakes.com

 Published by Lydia Inglett Ltd. Publishing
www.lydiainglett.com
301 Central Ave. #181
Hilton Head Island, SC 29926
info@starbooks.biz

share a slice of love!

Daisy Cakes

Fabulous heirloom cake recipes, Southern stories, and a pie or two, from the heart and kitchen of the Queen of Cakes – Kim Daisy and Daisy Cakes

SUGAR

KIM DAISY

LI
LTD
Lydia Inglett Ltd. Publishing

Contents

Welcome!

When fresh and sunny Kim Daisy stepped onto the *Shark Tank* set a few short years ago, everyone there was smitten by her Southern belle charm. Then we tasted her homemade cakes! While the boys were busy gobbling down cake, I stepped in and made a deal with Kim and her fledgling Daisy Cakes delivery business. I can safely say a sweeter deal has never been struck on the *Shark Tank* set!

Since that day, Kim has become not only a colleague but also a trusted friend, and her cakes have become nothing less than a staple in both my home and my office. Birthdays are sweeter with Kim's red velvet cake, a Southern favorite. Holidays always call for a classic 4-layer chocolate cake or a mouth-watering lemon cake with homemade lemon curd filling—or maybe both. And I'll use any excuse to order my own favorite, the moist, golden carrot cake that's topped off with the best cream cheese frosting I've ever tasted!

Kim Daisy knows her way around the kitchen like nobody's business. Of course that's not really surprising since she learned to cook at her grandmothers' and great aunt's apron strings. As a child, Kim liked nothing better than spending time in the kitchen, stirring together the farm fresh ingredients her grandmothers insisted on, licking the spoon after her great aunt Daisy mixed a batch of creamy frosting, and along the way learning how these great Southern women made the desserts they were known for countrywide. Pretty soon, Kim was whipping up her own desserts, hand sifting the flour and icing the cakes with sweet cream frosting just like her grandmas and aunt before her.

Kim put the same loving care as she puts into every cake she bakes into creating this, her first cookbook. In these pages she shares treasured family recipes for cakes, pies, and puddings, and the key to making that just right, not-too-sweet, cream cheese frosting. Along the way she tells just what it was like growing up around her grandmothers Miss Nellie and Miss Nervielee and her great aunt Daisy. Turn the page to learn their secrets to making authentic, blue ribbon winning cakes and desserts.

Happy baking!

- Barbara Corcoran

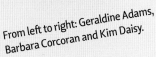

From left to right: Geraldine Adams, Barbara Corcoran and Kim Daisy.

Into the Shark Tank!

One warm June day in 2010, a friend phoned to tell me about a new ABC TV show called *Shark Tank* that featured entrepreneurs pitching their business to potential investors. (Back then, I only knew of a shark tank as a place where marine biologists and really brave tourists went to view great whites in the ocean.) I checked out the ABC website and found a section for *Shark Tank* casting and decided to upload my information: name, age, website, product description and a picture. What they wanted was simple. I thought the process would be simple too. It soon became obvious that this would not be the case as I was about to be introduced to the world of reality television.

Within twenty four hours of uploading my information, I got a call! It was late afternoon. I was out walking my dog, Daisy. An unusual number appeared on my phone. Oh my goodness! It was the casting coordinator calling to tell me that I was being considered as a "possible" entrepreneur for the show! I was so excited that I ran all the way home. Completely out of breath, I called Mama. We had to ship some cakes to Los Angeles right away!

My mother met me at the UPS hub with the cakes. I wrote a hurried thank-you note to the casting lady, put it in the box with the cakes and off they went. Little did we know we'd be shipping out the most important cakes of our life.

Over the course of the summer, I was assigned two producers from the show, Bill and Laura, who were instrumental in helping me with my pitch. We had several phone calls with executives from the show who listened to my story and business plan. It was a fun, exciting and certainly stressful ride. By the way, I still had no idea if I'd be chosen for the show.

Finally, nearly three months later, I got the call I was waiting for! I was approved to make the

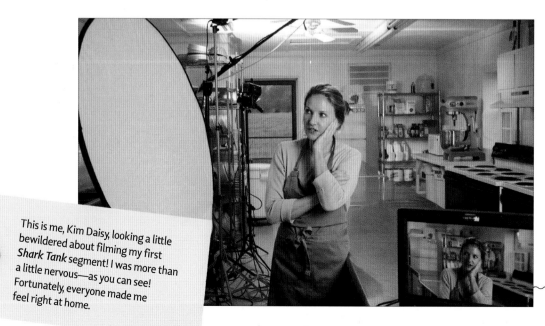

This is me, Kim Daisy, looking a little bewildered about filming my first *Shark Tank* segment! I was more than a little nervous—as you can see! Fortunately, everyone made me feel right at home.

formal application to appear on *Shark Tank*. There was a twenty-seven page application to be filled out accompanied with a four-minute video. I only had six days to get it compiled and in their hands. No sweat, right? But it was all worth it when I got the call on October 27 notifying me that my plane was leaving the next morning at 11:00am.

After a whirlwind of work-related activity and packing, I was off to the airport and landing at LAX a few hours later. Upon arriving at the hotel, the first thing that caught my eye was how many other entrepreneurs were there as well. We congregated in the lobby, sharing stories, laughing and attempting to keep each other loose for rehearsals.

For the rehearsals, we were taken to the *Shark Tank* set on the Sony Pictures Studio lot in Culver City, the oldest studio lot in Hollywood. The original *King Kong* movie was filmed there in 1933. Six years later, the set was used for the burning of Atlanta scene from *Gone with the Wind*. It's currently home to many shows, including *Wheel of Fortune*. After spotting a photo of South Carolina's own Vanna White, I attempted to take a picture. A security guard swiftly interrupted and informed me that this was a "no photo zone". I simply replied, "Oh I am so sorry. I know it will be just fine because Vanna is from South Carolina and so am I!"

At 5:30am on Halloween morning, our group loaded into a van

for our taping. My private dressing room featured a large sofa, chair and mirror (for practicing). There was a delicious spread of food and drinks. The best part was the hair and makeup team who made me feel just like a movie star!

If you're reading this book, there's a good chance you've seen my eight-minute pitch from the show. (In reality, my pitch lasted forty-five minutes.) I spent 4 hours in my dressing room before it was my turn to go over to the set. After having my hair and makeup touched up and my microphone secured, the doors into the tank opened. I could hear the laughter of the sharks as I made my way down the long hallway. Once inside, I stood on my mark and waited for what felt like an eternity. I thought I was going to explode! As soon as the director gave me my cue, I served the sharks a slice of cake. The rest is history. I walked out of the tank with my perfect business partner, mentor and friend, Barbara Corcoran.

I am fortunate to have grown up in the South in a loving and supportive family. We all love being together and enjoying great food. It is because of my love of baking and my fabulous experience on *Shark Tank* that I am able to share some stories and recipes with you. I hope you enjoy them all.

The *Shark Tank* set is on the oldest studio lot where the original *King Kong* movie was filmed AND the lot where *Wheel of Fortune* is filmed.

Having fun with Barbara at our *Shark Tank* Retreat. She is a great business inspiration and mentor— even on a bicycle!

Fresh from the Kitchen

"You don't have to cook fancy or complicated masterpieces— just good food from fresh ingredients." -Julia Childs

Hey y'all! Welcome to the family! The story of Daisy Cakes wasn't born with a television appearance on *Shark Tank* or in our relatively new commercial kitchen. Our story dates back generations, with friends and family who had a passion for cooking and baking using farm-fresh ingredients.

Growing up in rural South Carolina, I spent a good bit of time in the kitchen and working with food. I can vividly remember the smells of freshly-baked cakes wafting through the air in Pauline. Our town was named for the daughter of our first postmaster in 1890 and features mostly farmland and pastures. The nearby city of Spartanburg features charming antebellum homes and brick storefronts, where there is never a lack of Southern grace.

Cooking and eating food that was picked directly from the garden has been a constant in my life. I knew the names of all our chickens which provided eggs for our breakfast every morning and were baked into our cakes. I watched seeds develop into carrots which were eventually added to our carrot cakes. I picked fresh pecans and gathered the eggs which were eventually added to pies. These experiences fostered my passion for fresh food.

For us in the South, cooking and baking is all about creating something together and sharing in the love. Throughout this book, I'll introduce you to my family and friends and share their recipes. First, I want to tell you about the special women in my life, who loved to cook and bake more than anything. They are the ones who instilled a love of fresh food in me and taught me the joy of preparing food for others and doing it the right way.

Before ... and AFTER!
It all started right here! My lifelong love affair with cakes and cooking began with an innocent chocolate cake!

A Heritage of Love, Great Women and Great Food

I want to tell you about the women who taught me not only how to cook but so much more. They taught me about really living ... love of family, sharing with one another, good, nourishing food and how to bake great cakes!

The special ladies in my life are: my grandmother, **Miss Nellie**, my mother's mother; my grandmother, **Miss Nervielee**, my father's mother; my great aunt, **Miss Daisy**; and of course my mother, **Miss Geraldine**. You can learn more about our family from the Daisy Cakes' Family Tree on page 128.

In the South we call all the ladies "Miss," regardless of their age or martial status. It's a term of endearment and respect. It's very telling when you hear two women of the same age calling each other "Miss," as it shows that they really respect each other.

My cake company, Daisy Cakes, is inspired and named after Aunt Daisy who was a fabulous baker. She taught me how to bake and how to enjoy life and laugh! The company celebrates her life every day.

My grandfather, John Bishop, or Papa Bishop, was married to Miss Nellie. His sister Daisy was married to Jamie Bishop. John and Jamie weren't related; they just shared the same last name. They all lived together on a hilltop farm in Union, SC, in gentle harmony all their lives, sharing the upkeep of the farm, their meals and lots of laughs along the way.

The farm on top of the hill, as we referred to it, was a beautiful place. The road to the farm was

Miss Nervielee

Miss Nellie

Miss Daisy

Sunday dinner after church.

Top: My grandparents "house on the hill."
Bottom: The back porch where the long-handled drinking cup hung by the sink.

across a rickety bridge and up a steep dirt road. I always held my breath going over that bridge! At the top of the hill the road opened out to a large green field with centuries-old trees, the houses and barns and the pastures beyond.

Miss Nellie and Miss Daisy were inseparable. They began and ended each day together in their shared goals of caring for their husbands and families, cooking, working around the house and on the farm.

The main house where Miss Nellie and her husband lived was a white, clapboard house with an L-shaped screened porch. Many pleasant evenings were spent on that porch. After supper, the ladies and their husbands would retire to the glider swing and rocking chairs to rest and talk over the day, the running of the farm and what tomorrow might hold.

There was a sink near the door for washing up and on the wall beside the faucet hung a unique, long-handled metal cup. In the hot summer, after a day of playing in the fields and climbing trees, we kids would fling open that screen door, grab the long-handled cup, and take a deep cool drink, made cooler by the metal of the cup. I have such

fond memories of many days and weeks spent at the farm on the hill.

After relaxing on the porch together for a while, Miss Daisy and her husband would retire to bed in the "playhouse." Now, the playhouse got its name because my grandfather (Papa Bishop) built it for my mother, Miss Geraldine, and her sister, Miss Bobbie Ruth, when they were little girls. Years later, Miss Daisy and Jamie moved into the playhouse. It was a real house, just on a smaller scale with running water and electricity, but everyone continued to refer to it as the "playhouse."

Everyone at the farm rose early to meet the day. Miss Nellie and Miss Daisy would get into the kitchen to start cooking breakfast. And what a breakfast it was! Miss Nellie made her famous biscuits and started the Luzianne coffee, while Daisy started the bacon and sausage frying in the big, old black frying pan seasoned from years of use. Once the bacon and sausage were cooked, Daisy would cook the fresh eggs in the grease left in the big pan.

At 6:30am, Papa Bishop and Jamie would come in for breakfast. By this time of the morning they had worked up a big appetite. They had already

Daisy enjoying some springtime flowers.

A picnic in the mountains.

Celebrating Daisy's birthday. Mama Bishop is making gravy at the stove.

completed the morning farm chores. This included milking the cows, "slopping" the pigs and bringing the milk into the kitchen for the ladies to churn into butter. As the butter would come to the top of the churn, it would be scraped off and pressed into the pretty butter molds to harden.

After a big breakfast, the men went to work at the cotton mill in town. The ladies would clean up the breakfast dishes and discuss their plans for supper. First though, they had to feed their chickens which always included some day-old biscuits or cornbread. Their hens would cluck away over the scraps of crumbled bread.

Miss Nellie and Miss Daisy each had their own chicken pen. There was a spirit of friendly competition between them over whose chickens laid the most and the prettiest eggs. I remember one summer when Miss Daisy's chickens were not laying many eggs. Over in Miss Nellie's chicken pen, the hens were laying plenty of eggs. For several mornings in a row, Miss Daisy would hurry out to the chicken pens while Miss Nellie was finishing up the dishes. Miss Daisy would take one of her "non-laying" hens and switch it over to Miss Nellie's pen. Miss Daisy would then take one

of Miss Nellie's "laying" hens in exchange. This was done all in good fun. This hen swap went on for a few days until I just couldn't keep it a secret any longer. I had to tell it. We laughed and laughed and wondered how long it would have taken Miss Nellie to figure it out.

With the hens all fed and happy and eggs gathered from the nests, it was time to do a little laundry and work in the garden. The laundry was hung out to dry in the clean air year 'round. I can still remember that smell when I would help bring in the laundry from the clothesline. I would bury my face in the clothes, close my eyes and breathe—so fresh! There is nothing like it.

Once the animals were tended and the laundry hung, the ladies moved to the garden to weed, hoe and gather vegetables and fruit. There was always something growing at the farm on the hill. The summer garden had peas, carrots, okra, squash, tomatoes of all shapes, zucchini and cucumbers. Strawberries, blackberries and muscadines were made into jelly. Corn was grown in the fields and picked fresh for the table. Summertime vegetables were canned and then stored in the root cellar so they could be enjoyed in the

A birthday cake for Mama Bishop.

My oldest child Adam with Grandmommy Geraldine getting a lesson on icing a cake.

wintertime. In the fall, collards, spinach, mustard greens and lettuces were planted and enjoyed until spring planting time came back around. Nutritious, homegrown food was just normal back then. A high value was placed on good nutrition. It was a necessity for energy and health. Today some folks see fresh grown food as something special. I guess, in a way, it is.

Back inside the kitchen, conversation turned to what to bake. The ladies liked to have a little fun and would try to outdo each other with cakes and pies. Having fresh-baked sweets was a way they showed their husbands how much they loved them. In turn, the men would pay compliments to the ladies that showed they cared, not just about their cakes, but about them. It was a subtle way of expressing love and a treat after a long day's work.

The day passed quickly. Because Miss Nellie never learned to drive, each day Miss Daisy would drive to the mill at 3:00pm to pick up the men. Once home, Papa Bishop and Jamie would milk the cows, "slop" the pigs and tend to the smokehouse when hams were curing. The men always enjoyed a full supper every evening, kind of like the Sunday dinners we have nowadays. There were more fresh-baked biscuits, maybe some cornbread,

at least one meat dish depending on the season, gravy and a few vegetables from the garden. After supper came the reward for the day—a fresh-baked pie or cake served with coffee.

Miss Nellie and Miss Daisy enjoyed all their cooking, but they particularly enjoyed making desserts. They knew the recipes by heart from making them so many times. Thankfully for us, they wrote them down. I have their original handwritten recipes. I treasure them! When I reread them, I can hear my grandmother and aunt telling me how to work with the batter or the crust as they patiently taught me their secrets.

The eggs that went into their cakes and pies were fresh from the chickens. The milk was fresh from the cows and the butter freshly churned. We use farm fresh eggs in our Daisy Cakes today. We believe the chickens are happier and lay better tasting eggs.

The sisters-in-law relied on one another with ease and grace, always respectful and full of humor. Miss Daisy had a mischievous streak and liked to tell a joke and tickle us kids. She also enjoyed playing a prank every now and then. Miss Nellie was easily spooked. Papa Bishop loved to tell the story of riding his horse up the hill one evening, just as it was getting dark. He could see

Ma-Ma Adams, next to one of her many gigantic cabbages.

My cousins Jeff and Lydia Inglett and me (on the left) with Ma-Ma Adams. Looks like Jeff was the birthday boy!

Miss Nellie standing at the back gate. Miss Nellie didn't see him. Papa Bishop said, "Evenin' Nell." Being the fearful type, she fainted. I still laugh at this story. Mama Bishop lived to be ninety-four years old. She would be very proud of her daughter, Geraldine, and me for starting a cake business using some of her recipes.

Miss Daisy lived to be ninety-three years of age. She was an encouragement to me in everyday living as well as baking and cooking. She would be pleased about the company named in her honor and about the quality of cakes that we bake.

My father, R. T. "Rock" Adams' mother, Miss Nervielee, (Ma-Ma Adams to us grandkids), was another great influence in my life. Her mother gave her an unusual name, which she disliked. People who knew her would call her "Nervy," which she disliked even more! Now, people simply change their name but not back then. Nervy would tell people to call her Leigh.

Miss Nervielee also has a daughter, Mary Inglett, who is the mother of my friend, cousin and publisher, Lydia Inglett.

Miss Nervielee grew up in a large family as many of those in the early 20th century did. She had five brothers and three sisters, though one whose name was Birdie died in 1903. Miss Nerv-

ielee often wore the hand-me-downs of her brothers, hand-sewn denim overalls and boys shirts. Her father, Mangus Turner, was one-half Cherokee Indian. He was a very tall, noble-looking man with dark hair and high cheekbones. He died of pneumonia while his wife, Miss Lily Turner, was pregnant with her youngest child, Henry Turner. Miss Nervielee was four years old.

Imagine having your husband die and leave you with seven children to feed and clothe while you are pregnant!

Though Great-Grandma Turner had little education, she was a sharp and extremely resourceful provider and businesswoman. I remember Miss Nervielee, telling us about growing up. She said her mother, Miss Lily, kept a cow and chickens and sold milk, butter and eggs to keep the family going. She kept accounts of her sales and profits and was the person folks in need would go to for help. She was an avid seamstress as well.

On Sundays, she cooked a large meal. There was always plenty to share with all who came to Miss Lily's home. In the kitchen she kept a big barrel of molasses, which the kids ate with biscuits each day.

Once during a flu epidemic, the whole household came down with the flu. Miss Lily took all the children's bedding downstairs so they could keep

Miss Nervielee with her younger brother, Henry Turner. Their mother, Miss Lily was pregnant with him when his father died. Henry and Miss Nervielee both loved the outdoors and enjoyed fishing, gardening and rambling in the fields and woods together throughout their lives.

Miss Nervielee grew the most beautiful Irises. Deep, dark purple and so velvety. She gave me some of the bulbs, which I planted in my front yard. Each spring I am reminded of her by these delicate, intensely colored flowers.

warm around the fire. She was so sick herself that the neighbors would leave food on the doorstep each day. Slowly they got better. In those days before antibiotics, the flu oftentimes meant death. The neighbors would not chance coming into the house to tend them.

Miss Lily lived to be ninety-seven years old. She was quite a woman. I'm honored to have known her. I have some of her hand-stitched quilts. I love to get them out and think about her extraordinary spirit.

Miss Nervielee was quite a tomboy as you can imagine growing up with five brothers. She could make a "cane" (bamboo) pole to fish with, shoot a gun, and hunt. Whatever those boys did, she did. She could run as fast as they could, with her long black hair flying in the wind—with bare feet!

One of her chores was to clean the pots and pans. Today we use a scrubby pad. But back then, she had to take the pots and pans outdoors and scrub them clean with sand!

Imagine! She swore that they would just gleam.

When I think of Ma-Ma Adams, a number of memories come to mind. She was such an inspiration! She was firm, but loving and very clean, and became a nurse later in life. Miss Nellie and Miss Daisy would let me pick the crust off the cakes or pinch a meringue top off, but not Ma-Ma Adams. Whenever I went to Ma-Ma's house, the first sound I usually heard was the hiss of the pressure cooker.

She worked with food with a reverence that I've not seen since. Her creamed corn is still the best I've ever tasted. Her secret was to only cut off the tip end of the corn, then scrape the cob to get all the "juice" out of the kernels.

Miss Nervielee's garden was like the *Land of the Giants*; the vegetables were so lush and abundant! She had a great interest in nutrition and taught me so much about healthy eating. She had a saying that I still use today, "Eat low to the ground." She also said, "You should have a little sugar ..." Did I mention that she made a mean banana pudding? My cousins and I would fight over who got to lick the pot and spoon of the homemade pudding. Yummy!

Miss Nervielee kept bees and would feed them. She did not smoke the bees or wear protective clothing when handling them because they didn't sting her. She had a way with animals, large or small. There was something really special about her that I think even the animals and bees could sense.

All of these women made me who I am today. I am so grateful! They taught me how to appreciate and use fresh ingredients to bake cakes full of fun and love. Their art form was food. They used it to express their love for their families and friends.

I am so proud of these strong, hard-working, big-hearted women. This is my heritage. I want to share it with you.

Cakes

SHARE A SLICE OF LOVE

Yellow Cake Layers

This basic layer cake can be spread with jam or filling and covered in frosting. Let it be your 'go-to' starting point on your baking adventure and it will always serve you well!

1½ cups sugar
½ cup shortening
2 eggs
2 cups sifted unbleached all-purpose flour (sift and then measure)
½ teaspoon salt
2¼ teaspoons baking powder
1 cup whole milk
1 teaspoon pure vanilla extract

Preheat the oven to 350 degrees. Grease and flour three 8-inch cake pans.

In the bowl of an electric stand mixer, cream together the sugar and shortening until fluffy. Add the eggs. Mix thoroughly.

Sift together the already sifted and measured flour with the salt and baking powder. Add the flour mixture to the mixing bowl, along with the milk and vanilla. Mix well. Scrape down the sides and around the bottom of the bowl. Mix well again, 1 minute on high speed.

Pour the batter into the prepared pans. Bake for 20-25 minutes, until golden and the cake is pulling away from the sides of the pans.

Cool the cake for 10 minutes and remove from the pan. You can put a filling between the cake's layers or icing between the layers and on the outside of the cake.

Hint: Freezing your cake layers makes it so much easier to spread the filling and icing on them. Freezing them for 2-3 hours is a good length of time.

Serves: 12-16 people

Apple Pecan Cake

In our eyes, autumn couldn't begin until *The Ladies* had their annual apple picnic. Each year we would designate a weekend in the fall to make our pilgrimage to the mountains, filled with laughter, baking and, of course, delicious apples. After stuffing our picnic basket and loading up the car, Miss Geraldine would drive us to the picnic site that our family had been going to for ages. The table sat along the roadside and you could hear the running water of the stream in the background as you finished up lunch. We piled back into the car and eventually arrived at the orchard for the annual apple tasting. We tasted every type of apple that the grower had. Finally, we decided on two bushel boxes of Winesap apples, which we believed to be the best for both eating and baking. We loaded the boxes of apples into the trunk of the car. We couldn't wait to get back home to begin baking.

1¼ cups canola oil
2 cups sugar
3 eggs
3 cups unbleached all-purpose flour
1 teaspoon baking soda
1 teaspoon salt
2 teaspoons pure vanilla extract
4 apples (firm & sweet), peeled and finely chopped
1 cup toasted pecans

Whisk together the oil and sugar. Add the eggs, beating well. Sift the dry ingredients together and fold into the egg mixture. Stir in the vanilla, apples and pecans.

Pour the apple mixture into a greased and floured 9 x 13 x 2-inch glass baking dish. Bake at 350 degrees for 40-45 minutes. Pour the glaze over the cake while warm.

GLAZE
1 cup sugar
½ teaspoon baking soda
½ cup buttermilk
1 tablespoon corn syrup
¼ cup (½ stick) unsalted butter
1 teaspoon pure vanilla extract

Combine the sugar, baking soda, buttermilk, corn syrup and butter. (Use at least a 2-quart pan, as the sugar mixture bubbles up during cooking.)

Cook the sugar mixture over medium heat until the soft ball stage. Remove from heat. Add the vanilla. Pour over the cake and let cool.

Serves: 12-16 people

Tasty & Moist!
This cake is very moist! It keeps well and goes great with coffee.

SHARE A SLICE OF LOVE

Black Walnut Cake

1 cup (2 sticks) unsalted butter,
at room temperature
⅓ cup shortening
2 ½ cups sugar
5 eggs
2 ½ cups cake flour
1 teaspoon baking powder
¼ teaspoon salt
1 cup whole milk
1 cup black walnuts

Preheat the oven to 300 degrees. Grease and flour a 10-inch tube pan.

In the bowl of an electric stand mixer, cream the butter, shortening, and sugar until light and fluffy. Add the eggs. Beat well. Scrape down the sides and around the bottom of the bowl.

Sift together the flour, baking powder, and salt. Add to the butter mixture along with the milk. Blend. Scrape down the sides and around the bottom of the bowl. Mix on high for 2 minutes. Add the walnuts. Blend. Pour the batter into the prepared tube pan. Bake 1½ hours. DO NOT OPEN THE DOOR!

Serves: 16-20 people

Miss Nervielee's Plain Pound Cake

Miss Nervielee, or Ma-Ma Adams as I called her, had a special way of working with food. Healthy, nourishing food was important after a hard day's work. Her famous pound cake has a divinely crisp outer crust that crunches when you bite into it. It was so good that we children would sneak pieces of that crust when no one was looking.

1 cup (2 sticks) unsalted butter, at room temperature
½ cup shortening
3 cups sugar
5 eggs
3 ¼ cups unbleached all-purpose flour
½ teaspoon baking powder
¼ teaspoon salt
1 cup whole milk
3-5 teaspoons vanilla extract or your favorite flavor(s)

Preheat the oven to 325 degrees. Grease and flour a 10-inch tube pan.

In the bowl of an electric stand mixer, cream together the butter, shortening, and sugar until light and fluffy. Scrape down the sides and around the bottom of the bowl. Add the eggs. Mix well. Scrape down the sides and around the bottom of the bowl. Mix on high speed for 2 minutes.

Sift together the flour, baking powder, and salt; add to the butter mixture along with the milk and vanilla extract. Mix on low to combine. Scrape down the sides and around the bottom of the bowl. Mix on high for 2 minutes. Pour the batter into the prepared pan. Bake for 65-75 minutes, or until the cake tester comes out with just a few crumbs.

Cool the cake for 20 minutes before turning out onto a cake plate.

Serves: 16-20 people

Nervielee's Blue Hydrangeas
These cheery flowers, seen on opposite page, were always grown on the side of her house. The profusion of vivid blue is one of nature's loveliest colors.

25

SHARE A SLICE OF LOVE

Miss Daisy's Plain Pound Cake

Miss Daisy and Miss Nervielee each had their favorite pound cake recipe. Never ones to be outdone, they would occasionally try, in a friendly way, to get folks to say that their particular pound cake was the best. Now, of course, folks will say most anything for a fresh slice of just baked cake! Try baking one of each and ask your friends and family to pick their favorite.

1 cup shortening
¾ cup (1 ½ sticks) unsalted butter, at room temperature
3 cups sugar
6 eggs
3 cups cake flour
½ teaspoon salt
¾ cup whole milk
2 tablespoons pure vanilla extract

Preheat the oven to 350 degrees. Grease and flour a 10-inch tube pan.

In the bowl of an electric stand mixer, cream together the shortening, butter, and sugar until light and fluffy. Add the eggs. Blend. Scrape down the sides and around the bottom of the mixing bowl. Mix on high for 1 minute.

Sift together the flour and salt. Add the flour to the butter mixture along with the milk and extract. Blend. Scrape down the sides and around the bottom of the mixing bowl. Mix on high for 2 minutes.

Pour the batter into a prepared tube pan and bake at 350 degrees for 65-70 minutes.

Cool the cake for 20 minutes before turning out onto a cake plate.

Serves: 16-20 people

How Did The Pound Cake Get Its Name?

The name "Pound Cake" is so named because originally it contained a pound each of four ingredients: flour, butter, eggs and sugar. Today this would make a cake much larger than most families can consume and has changed over time.

Many countries have a version of what we know as pound cake. In France, since the French do not use the pound unit of measure, the cake is called Quatre-Quarts, which means four-fourths, and is made using quarts of the four main ingredients.

Our recipes have been adapted over the generations, but the great taste and wholesome goodness of a pound cake, whether dressed up or plain, is still tops in our book!

Miss Daisy's Plain Pound Cake

Here is Miss Daisy's handwritten recipe for her pound cake. I have kept it in my recipe drawer for over thirty years. Whenever I read over her recipes, I can hear her instructing me as to how to work with the ingredients to get the batter just right. I hope that you will try making it and then judge for yourself!

Plain Cake

1 cup Crisco
1½ stick of Margarine
3 cups sugar
6 eggs
3/4 cups sweet milk

3 cups cake flour

¼ teaspoon ~~salt~~

3 tablespoons vanilla or
lemon
Cook one hour
350 — start in cold oven.

Cream Crisco and margarine and sugar
togather, then add eggs, beat well
Add milk, then flour, salt
and flaoring.

Chocolate Zucchini Cake

For six years, I had a cooking school, *Cooking Up a Storm*. It started when Miss Lee Ann's son, tired of eating out every single day, pleaded with his mother, "Mama, please ask Miss Kim to teach you how to cook so we can eat at home." My friend Lee Ann gave me a handwritten card that read, "Each of you should use whatever gift you have received to serve others, as faithful stewards of God's grace in its various forms." I Peter 4:10 So it began! The students were given the recipes for each four-week session. Over the years, more than 300 students came in with their ingredients and left with dinners that they had prepared ready for the following nights at home.

One student, Julie, was not born to cook. She was bravely taking cooking classes to be with some of her girlfriends and to have supper at home for her family a few nights each week.

One beautiful fall day, we were making two dinner casseroles and this zucchini cake. A lot of eggs were involved in all three recipes. After everyone's cakes were in the ovens, Julie asked, "Why do I have all these extra eggs?" She had forgotten to put the eggs into her cake batter! Surprisingly, the cake actually held together and turned out of the pan quite well. It even tasted fine. So, you can make this cake and leave out the eggs. Julie did!

1 cup (2 sticks) unsalted butter, at room temperature
1 cup sugar
1 cup light brown sugar (packed)
8 ounces cream cheese, room temperature
4 squares (1-ounce each) unsweetened chocolate, melted and cooled
2 tablespoons unsweetened cocoa powder
6 eggs
1 orange, all of the zest and juice
2¾ cups unbleached all-purpose flour
1 teaspoon salt
1 teaspoon baking powder
1 teaspoon baking soda
2 cups semisweet chocolate chips
3 cups grated zucchini, squeeze out excess liquid

Preheat the oven to 350 degrees. Grease and flour a 12-cup Bundt pan.

In a large mixing bowl, cream together the butter and both sugars until light and fluffy. Add the cream cheese, melted chocolate, and cocoa. Beat for 2 minutes. Add the eggs, orange zest, and juice. Scrape down the sides and around the bottom of the mixing bowl.

Sift together the flour, salt, baking powder and baking soda. Add the flour mixture to the butter and sugar mixture and beat on low until blended. Fold in the chocolate chips and zucchini. Pour the batter into the Bundt pan. Bake for 60-65 minutes, or until an inserted skewer comes out with just a few crumbs on it.

Cool the cake for about 20 minutes before turning out of the pan.

Serves: 16-20 people

SHARE A SLICE OF LOVE

Citrus Poppy Seed Cake

Are you a citrus lover? Then you will love this cake! You can use your favorite citrus fruit. If I'm not having chocolate, then make mine citrus!

½ cup (1 stick) unsalted butter, at room temperature
1½ cups sugar
4 eggs
2 cups unbleached all-purpose flour
2½ teaspoons baking powder
½ teaspoon salt
¾ cup whole milk
½ cup poppy seeds
1 teaspoon pure vanilla extract
The zest of either: 2 oranges, 2 lemons, 2 limes, 4 tangerines, or 4 clementines

Preheat the oven to 325 degrees. Grease and flour a 10-inch Bundt pan.

In the bowl of an electric stand mixer, cream together the butter and sugar until light and fluffy. Add the eggs. Mix well.

Sift the flour, baking powder, and salt together. Add to the creamed mixture along with milk. Mix. Scrape down the sides and bottom of the bowl. Mix on high speed for 1 minute.

Fold in the poppy seeds, vanilla, and zest. Pour the batter into the prepared pan.

Bake for 50-60 minutes, or until the inserted skewer comes out with just a few crumbs on it.

When the cake comes out of the oven, poke holes in the cake. Pour the glaze over the cake while the cake is still in the Bundt pan. Cool the cake for about 30 minutes before turning out onto a cake plate.

GLAZE
½ cup fresh orange juice, or other citrus juice
½ cup sugar
2 tablespoons (¼ stick) unsalted butter

Combine the juice, sugar, and butter in nonreactive saucepan. Whisk and simmer gently until the sugar dissolves and the sauce reduces to a light syrup. Pour the glaze over the warm cake while the cake is still in the pan.

Hint: When using limes or lemons, increase the sugar amount to 1 cup.

Serves: 16-20 people

SHARE A SLICE OF LOVE

Apple-Walnut Pound Cake

I loved gathering eggs with Miss Nellie and Miss Daisy. I would carefully take the fresh eggs from each nest. The eggs were still warm when we collected them. It was fun knowing they would make a delicious cake. Nowadays, we consider farm fresh eggs a luxury. When I was growing up I thought everyone had them. I loved to call the hens by name, pet them and thank them for giving us such lovely eggs.

2 cups sugar

1 1/2 cups canola oil

3 eggs

3 cups unbleached all-purpose flour

1 teaspoon baking soda

1 teaspoon salt

1 tablespoon pure vanilla extract

3 cups apples, peeled and diced

1 cup black walnuts

1 cup coconut

Preheat the oven to 350 degrees. Grease and flour a 10-inch tube pan.

In a large mixing bowl, whisk together the sugar, oil, and eggs until well blended and light yellow in color.

Sift together the flour, baking soda, and salt. Add the flour mixture and the vanilla to the mixing bowl with the oil and sugar mixture. Whisk well. The batter will be very stiff. Fold in the apples, black walnuts, and coconut.

Pour the batter into a prepared 10-inch tube pan. Bake for 1 hour 20 minutes.

Let cool in the pan for 20 minutes before turning out onto the cake plate.

Serves: 16-20 people

34

Cherry Cake

Henry Turner was one of Miss Nervielee's brothers. He served our country during World War II and was stationed at Pearl Harbor when it was attacked by Japanese planes on the 7th of December 1941. At the end of World War II, the Allied Powers occupied Japan from 1945-1952. Uncle Henry brought back the tea set shown at the right. It is stamped "Made in Occupied Japan" and is a family heirloom.

2½ cups sifted cake flour (sift first and then measure)
1½ cups sugar
3½ teaspoons baking powder
1 teaspoon salt
½ cup shortening
¾ cup whole milk
¼ cup maraschino cherry juice
1 teaspoon pure vanilla extract
2 teaspoons almond extract
4 egg whites, unbeaten
18 maraschino cherries well drained and finely chopped
½ cup pecans, chopped

Preheat the oven to 375 degrees. Grease and flour two 9-inch cake pans.

Sift together the flour, sugar, baking powder, and salt into a medium bowl. Drop in the shortening. Combine the milk and cherry juice. Add ¾ of the liquid and the extracts to the bowl.

Using an electric mixer, beat 200 strokes, or 2 minutes, on low. Add the remaining ¼ liquid and egg whites. Beat another 200 strokes or 2 minutes on low.

Fold in the cherries and pecans. Pour the batter into prepared pans and bake for 20-25 minutes. Cool completely before icing.

ICING

½ cup (1 stick) unsalted butter, at room temperature
1 teaspoon pure vanilla extract
½ teaspoon almond extract
Pinch of salt
6 cups powdered sugar
6-8 tablespoons scalded whipping cream

Cream the butter with the extracts, salt, and powdered sugar.

Add the milk slowly, a few tablespoons at a time, to make the icing into a nice consistency for spreading.

Spread over cooled cake.
Serves: 12-16 people

SHARE A SLICE OF LOVE

Creole Cake

Uncle George Bishop was an engineer for the railroad. He traveled around a good bit. He also liked to take hunting and fishing trips. Once while he was in Louisiana, he stayed with a Cajun family there and brought back this recipe as a gift from the lady of the house. Miss Nellie and Miss Daisy made the cake and it became an instant hit.

2 cups sugar
2 eggs
1/2 cup canola oil
1/2 cup buttermilk
2 cups unbleached all-purpose flour
2 tablespoons cocoa
1 teaspoon baking soda
1/4 teaspoon salt
1 teaspoon vanilla
1 cup boiling water

In large mixing bowl, whisk together the sugar, eggs, oil, and buttermilk. Fold in the dry ingredients: flour, cocoa, baking soda, and salt. Add the vanilla and boiling water. Blend all the ingredients together.

Pour the batter into a 9 x 13 x 2-inch glass baking dish. DO NOT GREASE THE DISH.

Bake at 325 degrees for 35-40 minutes.

TOPPING

1/2 cup (1 stick) unsalted butter, melted
1 cup light brown sugar (packed)
1 cup coconut
1/2 cup evaporated milk
1 cup pecans, chopped

Place the ingredients: butter, sugar, coconut, and evaporated milk in a small bowl and mix together well. Spread the topping on the cake as soon as it comes out of the oven. Sprinkle with pecans.

Return the cake to the oven for another 15 minutes, or until the topping is brown. Cut into squares in the pan and serve.

Serves: 12-16 people

David Muir and me along with a picture of the "Made in America" banner from the *ABC News* segment he did on Daisy Cakes.

SHARE A SLICE OF LOVE

Miss Nellie's Raisin Cake

My mother, Miss Geraldine, has fond memories of this raisin cake. Her grandmother, Granny Bishop, knew exactly how many sticks of wood to put in the stove to have the oven reach the correct temperature for baking. Miss Geraldine said she had to sit quietly at the table while the cake was baking for fear that any small movement would make the cake fall. She said she never understood what would make a cake fall, but she knew it would be awful to be responsible for such a thing.

Finally, the cake was done and pulled out of the oven. Once it was cool, Granny would put it on a large plate. The first slice of warm cake was always the best. Miss Geraldine says she can still smell that cake and remembers how good it was with a big glass of sweet milk from their very own cow.

1 cup (2 sticks) unsalted butter, at room temperature

½ cup shortening

½ cup (1 stick) margarine, at room temperature

1½ cups sugar

4 eggs

3 cups unbleached all-purpose flour

1 teaspoon baking powder

½ teaspoon salt

⅓ cup whole milk

1 teaspoon pure vanilla extract

2 cups raisins, place in a colander and dust lightly with flour

Preheat the oven to 250 degrees. Grease and flour a 10-inch tube pan.

In the bowl of an electric stand mixer, cream together the butter, shortening, margarine, and sugar. Add the eggs. Mix well. Sift together the dry ingredients. With the mixer on low, add the dry ingredients, milk, and vanilla extract to the butter mixture. Mix well. Scrape down the sides and around the bottom of bowl. Mix on high speed for 1 minute. Fold in the raisins. Put the batter into the prepared pan.

Bake for 2½ hours. Do not open the door or the cake will fall.

Serves: 12-16 people

Four generations celebrate Miss Nellie's (Mama Bishop's) 94th Birthday Celebration. Left to right: Kim Daisy, Nellie Bishop, Shelby Nelson and Geraldine Bishop Adams.

SHARE A SLICE OF LOVE

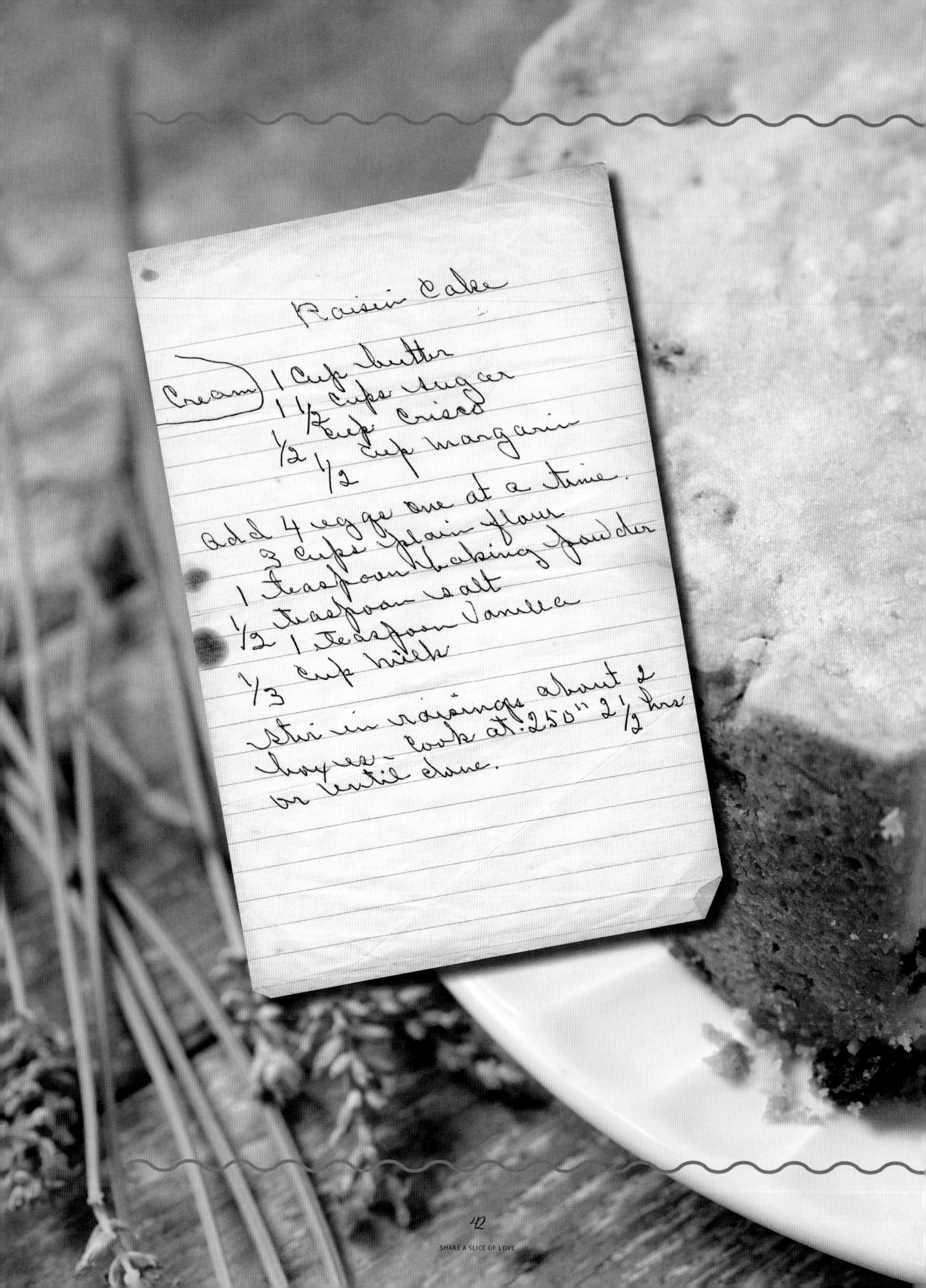

Raisin Cake

Cream) 1 cup butter
1 1/2 cups sugar
1/2 cup Crisco
1/2 1/2 cup margarin

Add 4 eggs one at a time.
3 cups plain flour
1 teaspoon baking powder
1/2 teaspoon salt
1/2 1 teaspoon vanilla
1/3 cup milk

Stir in raisings about 2
hoyes - Cook at 250" 2 1/2 hrs
or until done.

Chocolate Pound Cake

If you haven't tried a Chocolate Pound Cake, you simply must! The crumb texture along with the chocolate flavor make it an elegant dessert and a yummy late night snack.

1 cup (2 sticks) unsalted butter,
at room temperature
½ cup shortening
3 cups sugar
5 eggs
3 cups sifted unbleached all-purpose flour
(sift first and then measure)
½ cup cocoa
1 teaspoon baking powder
¼ teaspoon salt
1 cup whole milk
1 teaspoon pure vanilla extract

Preheat the oven to 350 degrees. Grease and flour a 10-inch tube pan.

In the bowl of an electric stand mixer, cream the butter, shortening, and sugar thoroughly. Add the eggs, one at a time, beating well after each.

Sift the already sifted flour with the cocoa, baking powder, and salt. Add the flour mixture to the butter mixture along with the milk and vanilla extract. Blend. Scrape down the sides and around the bottom of the bowl. Mix on high speed for 2 minutes.

Pour the batter into the prepared pan. Bake for 60 minutes. DO NOT OPEN THE OVEN DOOR!

Cool in the pan for 20 minutes before turning out onto the cake plate. Let cool completely before icing.

ICING
½ cup (1 stick) unsalted butter,
at room temperature
1 box powdered sugar
6 tablespoons cocoa
¼ - ½ cup evaporated milk
1 teaspoon vanilla extract

Cream the butter until smooth. Add the powdered sugar and cocoa, blending slowly.

Add ¼ cup of the evaporated milk and the vanilla extract. Mix well. Add more milk only if needed. Do not add too much milk or the icing will be too runny.

Spread over cooled cake.
Serves: 16-20 people

Lower Fairforest Baptist Church
Route 2
Union, South Carolina

GENE WHELCHEL
Pastor

MRS. RANDY WILBURN
Minister of Music

Enter to Worship - Depart To Serve

Homecoming Sunday

At Lower Fairforest Baptist Church in Union, South Carolina, you could always count on the pews being full on the last Sunday in August. That was Homecoming Sunday.

All the ladies would hurry around to get their signature dishes out on the tables under those big old oak trees. It was a beautiful sight. An array of fried chicken, ham, biscuits, fried okra, macaroni pie, fresh green beans, deviled eggs, sliced tomatoes and all kinds of homemade pickles covered the tables. These dishes came from farm to table when that was the only way these country cooks knew how to live.

Once it was all ready, Preacher Whelchel said the blessing and then it was time to eat.

I was always so proud when everybody wanted to know what my aunt and grandmother, Miss Daisy and Miss Nellie, had made. It didn't matter how many plates of biscuits, green beans or macaroni pie were on those tables. Miss Daisy's and Miss Nellie's fixin's were always the first to go.

45

Carrot Cake

Carrot Cake was probably first baked in Sweden. It became popular in Britain during the Second World War when sugar was rationed. Carrots contain almost as much sugar as beets and added a wonderful flavor to cakes. Carrot cake followed our troops home after the war and reached huge popularity in the 1960s when it showed up on restaurant menus. Our carrot cakes always have cream cheese icing. This carrot cake has a few more ingredients than our 24-Karat Cake. This cake was developed by my students during a cooking class at *Cooking Up a Storm*. I think you will enjoy baking and eating it as much as we enjoy sharing it with you.

2 cups unbleached all-purpose flour
1½ teaspoons baking soda
1 teaspoon baking powder
1 teaspoon cinnamon
¼ teaspoon salt
4 eggs
1½ cups canola oil
2 cups sugar
2 cups shredded carrots
8 ounces crushed pineapple, drained
1 cup coconut
½ cup chopped pecans

Preheat the oven to 350 degrees. Grease and flour two 9-inch round baking pans. Sift together the flour, baking soda, baking powder, cinnamon, and salt.

In a large mixing bowl, whisk together the eggs, oil, and sugar until well blended. Mix in the carrots, drained pineapple, coconut, and pecans. Add the sifted dry ingredients. Mix well.

Pour the batter into the prepared pans. Bake for 45-50 minutes, or until a skewer comes out clean. Cool completely before icing.

CREAM CHEESE ICING
1 cup (2 sticks) unsalted butter,
at room temperature
2 (8-ounce) packages cream cheese, cold
2 teaspoons pure vanilla extract
2 teaspoons fresh lemon juice
2 boxes powdered sugar

In the bowl of an electric stand mixer, cream the butter. Add the cream cheese, vanilla, and lemon juice. Add the powdered sugar. Mix well and spread on the cooled cake layers.

Hint: Make sure your mixer is on its lowest setting. (You will only have to learn this lesson one time.)

Serves: 16-20 people

This is similar to the recipe I prepared as one of the semi-finalists on ABC's *The Taste.*

Peach Cake from the *Today* Show

When I received the invitation to cook on the *Today* show, the big question was, "What should I cook?" I decided to make something with peaches since they are our state fruit. The Cooley family from Strawberry Hill sent the most perfect, juicy peaches from their farm in Gaffney, SC. This is the peach filling I made on the show. You can use it between the layers of my Yellow Cake recipe in the beginning of this book (page 10).

PEACH CAKE FILLING

12 ripe peaches, peeled and cut into small pieces
2 tablespoons sugar (or less) depending on the ripeness of the peaches
2 tablespoons fresh lemon juice
4 tablespoons peach gelatin, dissolved in
1/4 cup hot water

Mix all the ingredients; the peaches, sugar, lemon juice, and gelatin together in a medium-size bowl. Set aside.

Hint: Add 2 tablespoons peach gelatin (the dry powder) to the batter of your favorite yellow layer cake. Make into 4 layers.

Freeze the layers for two or three hours to make icing and assembling the cake easier.

ICING

3 cups heavy whipping cream
3 tablespoons powdered sugar

Chill the mixing bowl and whisk in the freezer for 15 minutes before using. Pour the heavy whipping cream and powdered sugar into a chilled bowl. Whip on high until stiff.

Reserve 2 cups of the whipped cream. Gently fold the remaining whipped cream into the peach filling.

Put the filling between the frozen cake layers, leaving about a 1-inch space around the edge. Assemble, leaving the top layer for the plain whipped cream. Cover the outside of the cake with plain whipped cream and top with any leftover peach filling. This cake is best when made one day ahead of time.

Serves: 8-12 people

Peaches Foster from the *Today* Show

There was a time when Spartanburg County produced more peaches than the entire state of Georgia. Around 1950, Spartanburg County had over three million peach trees and even out produced the large state of California in peach production. Peaches are the South Carolina State fruit and still a $40 million industry, producing some 60,000 tons of peaches each year.

½ cup (1 stick) unsalted butter
1 cup light brown sugar
6-8 ripe peaches, peeled and cut into wedges, not diced
½ cup brandy
cinnamon (optional)
toasted pecans (can be buttered and salted, if desired)

Melt the butter and brown sugar in a medium-size nonreactive pan. Add the peaches and cook until just heated through. Remove from the heat. Add the brandy and ignite. A sprinkle of cinnamon will add some sparkle to the flame. Serve over your favorite ice cream with toasted pecans.

Serves: 12-16 people

Chocolate Cherry Cake

This cake hits all the buttons! It's a satisfying combination of chocolate, coconut and cherry. Toasting the coconut changes its flavor entirely and adds a nice visual finish to the cake.

¾ cup (1½ sticks) unsalted butter, at room temperature
2 cups sugar
3 eggs
3 squares (1-ounce each) unsweetened chocolate, melted and cooled
3 cups sifted, unbleached all-purpose flour (sift and then measure)
1½ teaspoons baking soda
1 teaspoon salt
1½ cups whole milk
¼ cup maraschino cherry juice
12 maraschino cherries, sliced

Preheat the oven to 350 degrees. Grease and flour two 9-inch cake pans.

In the bowl of an electric stand mixer, cream together the butter and sugar until light and fluffy. Add the eggs. Beat well. Scrape down the sides and around the bottom of the bowl. Add the melted chocolate. Beat well.

Sift together the already sifted flour, baking soda, and salt. Add the flour mixture to the butter mixture along with the milk and cherry juice. Mix on low. Scrape down the sides and bottom of the mixing bowl. Continue mixing on high for 1 minute. Fold in the sliced cherries.

Pour the batter into prepared pans. Bake for 30-35 minutes. Let the cake layers cool in pans for 20 minutes before turning out onto the cake plate. Cool completely before icing.

ICING
1⅓ cups white corn syrup
2 egg whites
Pinch of salt
½ teaspoon almond extract
½ teaspoon pure vanilla extract
1 drop red food coloring (optional)
Coconut flakes, toasted

In a small pan, heat the corn syrup over low heat until boiling. In the bowl of an electric stand mixer, beat the egg whites until soft peaks form. Add the salt. While the mixer is on high, slowly pour the hot corn syrup into the bowl and continue beating the egg whites until they become a fluffy, glossy icing. Add the extracts. Tint the icing with a drop or two of food coloring. Put the icing on the cake layers. Sprinkle with coconut.

Serves: 12-16 people

SHARE A SLICE OF LOVE

Japanese Fruit Cake

This is a funny name for a cake that has, as far as we can tell, no connection to the Orient. We think Miss Nellie and Miss Daisy named it that because it seemed exotic to them all those years ago.

1 cup (2 sticks) unsalted butter,
at room temperature
2 cups sugar
4 eggs
3 cups unbleached all-purpose flour (sifted)
2 teaspoons baking powder
Pinch of salt
1 cup whole milk
1 teaspoon pure vanilla extract

Preheat the oven to 375 degrees. Grease and flour three 9-inch cake pans.

In the bowl of an electric stand mixer, cream together the butter and sugar until very creamy, light and fluffy. Add the eggs. Mix well.

Sift together the flour, baking powder and salt. Add the sifted ingredients, along with the milk and vanilla extract, to the mixing bowl with the butter and sugar mixture. Beat on high speed 2 minutes.

Put 2/3 of the batter into 2 of the prepared pans.

Into the remaining 1/3 of the batter, add:
1 teaspoon allspice
1 teaspoon cinnamon
1 teaspoon nutmeg
1 cup golden or regular raisins finely chopped and lightly dusted with flour

Put spice batter into the prepared pan.
Bake the layers for 20-25 minutes. Cool for 10 minutes and remove from the pans.

LEMON FILLING
1/2 cup (1 stick) unsalted butter,
melted and slightly cooled
1 cup sugar
6 egg yolks
2 lemons, zested and juiced

Whisk the butter and sugar together in the top of a double boiler. Add the yolks and lemon juice. Cook until thick, stirring constantly about 20 minutes. Cool the icing before spreading between the cooled cake layers.

WHITE ICING
2 egg whites
1 teaspoon baking powder
2 cups sugar
1 cup water
1 teaspoon white vinegar

In the bowl of an electric stand mixer, beat the egg whites until stiff. Add the baking powder.

Mix in the sugar, water and vinegar in a 2 qt. sauce pan and cook until the mixture comes to a good boil and spins a thread. Slowly add the sugar mixture to the egg whites and beat on high speed.

Continue beating until the icing is stiff enough to hold its shape. This icing will go on the outside of the cake.

To assemble: Place a plain cake layer on a cake plate. Spread one half of the lemon filling on the cake. Place the spice layer on top. Spread the remaining lemon filling on the spice layer. Top with a second plain cake layer.

Spread the white icing on the outside of the cake on both the top and sides.

Hint: The lemon filling can be sprinkled with fresh or frozen coconut if desired.

Serves: 16-20 people

Miss Geraldine's Italian Cream Cake

This is my mother's favorite cake. Her best friend, Mable, used to make this cake for us for special occasions. She would present it on a dome covered glass pedestal, swiftly removing the dome to *oohs* and *ahhs* of our family.

5 eggs, separated
1/2 cup (1 stick) unsalted butter,
at room temperature
1/2 cup shortening
2 cups sugar
1 teaspoon baking soda
1 cup buttermilk
2 cups unbleached all-purpose flour, sifted
two times
1 cup coconut
1 cup chopped pecans
1 teaspoon pure vanilla extract
1 teaspoon coconut extract

Preheat the oven to 350 degrees. Grease and flour three 9-inch cake pans.

Separate the eggs and beat the egg whites until stiff. Set aside.

Cream the butter and the shortening together. Add the sugar and beat until light and fluffy. Add the egg yolks. Mix well.

Dissolve the soda in the buttermilk. Add the flour to the egg and butter mixture along with the buttermilk. Beat well. Add the coconut, nuts, and extracts. Mix well. Fold in the stiffly beaten egg whites. Pour the batter into the prepared pans, using 2 cups of batter for each pan. Bake for 25 minutes. Cool for 15 minutes before turning out of the pan. Cool the layers completely before icing.

CREAM CHEESE ICING
1/2 cup (1 stick) unsalted butter,
at room temperature
1 package (8-ounces) cream cheese, cold
1 teaspoon almond extract
1 box powdered sugar

Cream the butter. Add the cream cheese. Mix well. Add the extract and powdered sugar. Beat until smooth. Spread the icing between the layers and on top of the cooled cake.

Serves: 12-16 people

How to make buttermilk
Measure 1 tablespoon of white vinegar into a one cup measuring cup. Fill to the top with whole milk to make one cup.

Sunday Lunch At The White House On The Hill

Miss Geraldine, my mother, recalls the great Sunday lunches after church at the white house on the hill in Union, South Carolina. Miss Nellie and Miss Daisy would start preparations on Saturday afternoon. Early Sunday morning they prepared the last things before going to church. After church they rushed home and amid a flurry of activity; the chicken pieces were fried in lard until they were crisp and delicious and the biscuits were popped into the oven.

Sunday was the day set aside for family and friends with plenty of food and rest, and not too much outdoor work.

Even during the war years, when food was rationed, the farm provided for all their needs. The work was hard, but the food was fresh, wholesome and delicious.

Mama and me with our Blue Ribbon Award from *Taste!* Gourmet Food Show for our "Love Dat Lemon Cake."

Miss Nervielee's Fruit Cake

I know! I know! Fruit cake!
You have got to be kidding me! But wait...

My grandmother, Miss Nervielee, gave me the recipe for this delicious fruitcake. Cutting up the fruits and nuts is the hardest part of making this cake that has a delightful texture and is not overly sweet. If you like, you can wrap the loaves in cheesecloth and pour a little bourbon or brandy over the cakes each day for a few days. This recipe will change your opinion of fruit cake!

2½ pounds candied cherries (green and red)
2½ pounds candied pineapple
2½ pounds pecans
2 cups (4 sticks) unsalted butter, at room temperature
4 cups sugar
14 eggs
5 cups unbleached all-purpose flour
1 teaspoon salt
1 cup orange juice
1 tablespoon pure vanilla extract
1 tablespoon lemon extract

Preheat the oven to 250 degrees. Thoroughly grease and flour two 10-inch tube pans or four standard size loaf pans.

Cut the candied fruit into small-diced pieces. Chop the pecans.

In the bowl of an electric stand mixer, cream together the butter and sugar. Add the eggs. Blend. Scrape down the sides and around the bottom of the mixing bowl. Mix well.

Sift together the flour and salt. Add the flour mixture to the butter mixture, along with the orange juice and both extracts. Blend. Scrape down the sides and around the bottom of the mixing bowl. Mix on high for 2 minutes.

At this point, the batter will need to go into a very large mixing bowl. Fold in the candied fruit and pecans.

Put the batter into 2 prepared tube pans. If there is extra batter, you can put it into a loaf pan.

Bake 3 hours. Do not open the oven door. Cool for 30 minutes before turning out onto a cake plate. These cakes keep well wrapped in foil.

Hint: This recipe is much easier if divided in half and made in two batches/mixings.

Each loaf will serve 8-10 people
Tube pan serves 16-20 people

Peach or Strawberry Pound Cake

After standing on the tailgate of my daddy's truck picking peaches in the hot August sun, my mother, Miss Geraldine, and I went straight home and baked the peach version of this good and really simple cake. Of course, we did eat a peach or two, fuzz and all, standing over the kitchen sink with the juice running down our arms and dripping off our elbows.

I love this cake with homemade vanilla ice cream on a thick slice that is still warm out of the oven.

1½ cups canola oil
2 cups sugar
3 eggs
1 tablespoon vanilla
3 cups self-rising flour
3 cups fresh (not frozen) sliced strawberries or peaches
1 cup toasted, chopped pecans

Preheat the oven to 350 degrees. Grease and flour a 10-cup Bundt pan.

Whisk together the oil, sugar, eggs, and vanilla. Whisk in the flour. The batter will be very stiff. Fold in the strawberries or peaches and pecans.

Pour the batter into the prepared Bundt pan. Bake for 60-65 minutes, or until an inserted skewer comes out with just a few crumbs on it. Cool in the pan for 15 minutes before turning out onto a cake plate.

Serves: 16-20 people

Angel Food Cake

Having grown up as a good Southern Baptist, it wouldn't be right to have a devil's food cake (page 66) and not have an angel food cake. Angel food cake is no more difficult than making a regular cake and really makes quite an impression when served. Don't be surprised when you get lots of compliments!

1¹/₂ cups egg whites, approximately 12 eggs
1 teaspoon cream of tartar
1¹/₂ cups sugar
¹/₂ teaspoon fresh lemon juice
¹/₂ teaspoon pure vanilla extract
1 cup sifted unbleached all-purpose flour
(sift and then measure)
¹/₄ teaspoon salt
Resift the flour twelve times (if in doubt or you lose count, sift 1 more time). Add the salt during the final sift. Set aside for later.

Beat the egg whites until foamy. Add the cream of tartar. Continue beating until the egg whites are stiff. Add the sugar a tablespoon or two at a time. Add the fresh lemon juice and vanilla. Slowly add the flour. Do not over mix.

Fold the batter into an ungreased 10-inch tube pan with a removable bottom.

Put into a cold oven. Set the oven temperature to 350 degrees. Bake 40 minutes from the time the cake goes into the oven. After 40 minutes, turn off the heat. DO NOT OPEN THE OVEN DOOR.

Leave the cake in the oven for an additional 15-20 minutes.

Cool before turning out onto a cake plate.
Serves: 16-20 people

HINT: Cold eggs separate best. Room temperature egg whites beat best. After separating your eggs, put the bowl containing the egg whites into warm water for 15 minutes.

63

SHARE A SLICE OF LOVE

Have a Tea Party!

One of our favorite things is to have a tea party!
All you need is a beautiful cake, fruit and tea, and you
have created an elegant occasion that is very simple.
Encourage your guests to dress up
and to wear hats!

Mary Alice's Devil's Food Cake

I'm an only child (and I wouldn't have had it any other way). One of the perks of being an only child was growing up in a neighborhood with lots of friends and being invited over to their houses for dinner quite often. One of my favorite families to visit for dinner was the Haithcocks, affectionately known as "the squirrel family." They ate dinner every night at 6:00pm. I still, to this day, find that a remarkable feat! Mary Alice Haithcock worked Monday through Friday, not getting home until 5:00 in the afternoon. But by 6:00pm, dinner was cooked and ready to eat.

I was especially happy when Mary Alice made her signature devil's food cake with shiny, white Dream Whip icing. I could never get enough of it! She would even let me run my finger through the icing on the cake to sneak a taste. It was an extra special treat to get to lick the beaters! I suggest making these devil's food layers and spreading them with some freshly-made whipping cream. But, if you're feeling truly nostalgic, why not whip up a box of Dream Whip and taste for yourself why Mary Alice's cake was so yummy. You can even lick the beaters!

3 (1-ounce) squares unsweetened chocolate
1/2 cup (1 stick) unsalted butter, at room temperature
2 1/2 cups light brown sugar (packed)
3 eggs
2 1/4 cups sifted cake flour, (sift first and then measure)
2 teaspoons baking soda
1/2 teaspoon salt
2 teaspoons pure vanilla extract
1/2 cup buttermilk
1 cup boiling water

Preheat the oven to 375 degrees. Grease and flour three 8-inch cake pans.

Melt the chocolate in a glass measuring cup in the microwave. Set it aside.

In the bowl of an electric stand mixer, cream the butter until soft and airy. Add the sugar and continue beating until light and fluffy. Add the melted chocolate. Blend together and add the eggs. Mix well.

Sift together the cake flour, baking soda, and salt. Add the flour mixture to the chocolate mixture, along with the vanilla and buttermilk. Add the boiling water. Scrape down the sides and bottom of the mixing bowl. Mix again for about 2 minutes. Pour the batter into prepared pans. Bake for 22-28 minutes. Do not overcook or the cake layers will be dry.

Cool in the pans for 10 minutes. Remove from the pans and put a filling or icing between the layers.

Serves: 12-16 people

Hint: For this recipe, you will need to sift the cake flour first. After sifting, measure out the 2 1/4 cups. The cake flour will be sifted, yet again, when you sift it with the baking soda and salt.

Pies

Southern Style Pie Dough

Miss Nellie and Miss Daisy taught me to roll pie dough. There was a big dough bowl where they would put the flour (unmeasured, of course), lard and ice water. The mixture was worked into a perfect dough. Flour was spread onto the counter and onto the rolling pin, then the dough was formed into a disk and rolled outwards from there. It didn't matter how much of a mess I made learning the rhythm to rolling dough, sitting up on my knees on the yellow wooden kitchen step stool. This was a skill to last a lifetime! Once you get used to making your own pie dough, you'll be able to make a pie quickly and easily.

1½ cups unbleached all-purpose flour
2 tablespoons sugar
½ teaspoon salt
3 tablespoon unsalted butter, cold
3 tablespoons lard, cold
6-8 tablespoons ice water

Combine the flour, sugar, and salt in a food processor. Pulse a time or two. Add the cold butter and lard. Pulse until the mixture is coarse like cornmeal. Add 2 tablespoons ice water. Pulse a few times. With the food processor running, add the ice water a tablespoon at a time until the dough forms into a ball. Put the dough on plastic wrap. Knead with the heel of your hand 5 or 6 times. Form the dough into a disk. Wrap and put in the refrigerator for 30 minutes. Roll out onto a well-floured surface. Don't forget to flour your rolling pin, too.

Makes one 9-inch pie.

Something So Special

When Granny Bishop passed, she bequeathed her wedding band to her granddaughter, my mother, Miss Geraldine. Miss Geraldine holds that ring dear above all things. She recalls as a child her grandmother slipping the ring off her finger and allowing her to try it on. Miss Geraldine didn't understand the significance of the ring then, but she felt in her child's heart that this was a special moment between grandmother and granddaughter.

Chess Pie

Chess Pie is a simple, Southern specialty. The origin of the pie is uncertain, but according to James Beard's *American Cookery*, the name may have come from the term 'pie chest' which is another name for pie safe, a cabinet where one could cool pies that had screens on the doors of the chest to keep out pests.

1 cup (2 sticks) unsalted butter, at room temperature
1 cup sugar
3 egg yolks + 1 egg white
1 tablespoon water
1 teaspoon cider vinegar
Pinch of salt
1 teaspoon vanilla extract
One 9-inch pie shell, unbaked

Preheat the oven to 350 degrees.

Cream together the butter and sugar until pale yellow and smooth. Add the eggs and egg white. Beat well, until foamy. Scrape down the sides and around the bottom of mixing bowl. Add the water, vinegar, salt, and vanilla extract and continue beating until smooth. Pour into an unbaked pie shell. Bake at 350 degrees for 45 minutes, or until firm.

Serves: 8 people

Michael Symon, Autor of **Carnivore** and other cookbooks and my friend Cassi (left) at the South Beach Wine & Food Show.

SHARE A SLICE OF LOVE

Coconut & Pineapple Pie

This pie is one for sharing! It is so easy to bake and so-o-o-o satisfying to serve and eat. It's Lydia's favorite recipe from her grandmother, Miss Nervielee: "When I would travel to Ma-Ma's house, it wasn't too long after I had gotten comfortable that I would gently ask her to make the coconut pie. She always went one better and made two pies! I can still close my eyes and imagine sitting down with her at the kitchen table to talk, laugh and eat warm pie." Try it and you'll see why!

4 eggs
2 cups sugar
1/2 cup (1 stick) unsalted butter, melted
1 tablespoon all-purpose flour
1 tablespoon cornmeal
1 can (8 ounces) crushed pineapple, undrained
3 ounces frozen coconut, thawed
1 teaspoon vanilla extract
Two 9-inch pie shells, unbaked
Sweetened coconut, toasted, for topping

Preheat the oven to 350 degrees.

Beat the eggs. Add the sugar, melted butter, flour, and cornmeal. Mix well. Fold in the crushed pineapple, thawed coconut, and vanilla extract. Pour into two 9-inch, unbaked, pie shells. Bake 45 minutes, or until firm. Sprinkle with toasted, sweetened coconut.

Serves: 8 people

Hint: If you like a pie with zing, add 2 teaspoons of rum extract to the filling.

Miss Nervielee always liked to buy her apples direct from the source. After smelling the fresh harvest available, she would pick out her apples and buy a bushel or two to take home. She made everything from canned applesauce and apple butter to pies and apple cake.

SHARE A SLICE OF LOVE

Miss Daisy's Chocolate Pie

Sunday dinner after church meant a table full of the best food you would ever put in your mouth! Two of my favorite desserts were the pound cake and Miss Daisy's Chocolate Pie. While Daisy was putting ice into the glasses and Mama Bishop was finishing up the gravy, I would pick the golden brown meringue peaks off the top of the pie. This was a sneaky act that took only a few seconds!

1½ cups sugar
½ cup cocoa
¼ cup cornstarch
3 eggs, separated, saving whites
for the meringue
¼ teaspoon salt
1 large can evaporated milk
2 teaspoons vanilla extract
¼ stick unsalted butter, melted
9-inch pie pastry, baked and cooled

Preheat the oven to 350 degrees.

In a medium-sized saucepan, whisk together the first six ingredients. Cook over low heat until thick, stirring constantly. Remove from heat. Add the vanilla extract and butter. Mix well. Pour into a baked and cooled 9-inch pie pastry crust. Top with meringue.

MERINGUE
Reserved egg whites
2 tablespoons sugar
1 tablespoon cream of tartar

Beat the egg whites until soft peaks form. Add 2 tablespoons sugar and 1 tablespoon cream of tartar. Spread over the chocolate filling. Bake in the oven for 12-15 minutes, or until brown .
Serves: 8-10 people

Buttermilk Pie

This recipe is very similar to chess pie. The ingredients are simple and ones that most kitchens have on hand. Miss Nellie and Miss Daisy always had fresh buttermilk, right from the churn, to use for their buttermilk pie. The rich depth of flavor that it gives is very pleasant and distinct.

2 tablespoons all-purpose flour
1½ cups sugar
3 eggs
½ cup unsalted butter, melted
Pinch of salt
½ cup good quality buttermilk
One 9-inch pie shell, unbaked

Preheat the oven to 350 degrees.

In a medium bowl, mix together the flour and sugar. Beat the eggs well . Add the melted butter, salt, and buttermilk to the eggs. Combine with the flour mixture and mix well. Pour into an unbaked pastry shell. Bake at 350 degrees about 40-45 minutes, or until the custard is set and the top is brown.

Serves: 8 people

Baton Rouge Annual Outing

Yes that's Darwell, the artiste and owner!

It's a long drive from Pauline, South Carolina, to Baton Rouge, Louisiana, fourteen hours to be exact. For four years in a row, Mama and I traveled that road to attend the Junior League of Baton Rouge's "Hollydays" to sell our Daisy Cakes.

Once we reached Mobile, Alabama, we knew it wouldn't be long before it was supper time. No place is more special to us than Darwell's Cafe in Long Beach, Mississippi. Since appearing on the TV show *Diners, Drive-Ins and Dives*, Darwell's has become insanely popular.

Darwell's is located by the railroad tracks. Darwell Yeager is full of fun and personality with an abundance of Southern charm. His food is some of the best Mama and I have ever eaten! Darwell is a talented caricature artist who doodles happily on each diner's styrofoam cup.

It was always hard to leave the great atmosphere, great food and live music. We had to hit the road again to see our friends in Baton Rouge. We plan on going back to Darwell's every year as long as "the good Lord is willing and the creek don't rise."

SHARE A SLICE OF LOVE

Pecan Pie

Any Southern cook, worth his or her weight, has a stash of pecans in their freezer. It's just as natural as having milk and eggs in the fridge. Cracking them and picking out the meat is no easy task. It sure is nice to have bags of pecans ready to use when you need them. They're good to eat cold, too.

3 eggs, beaten
½ cup sugar
2 tablespoons unsalted butter, melted
1 cup Karo syrup, light
1½ cups chopped pecans
1 teaspoon vanilla extract
Pinch of salt
9-inch pie shell, unbaked

Preheat the oven to 350 degrees.

Mix together the eggs, sugar, syrup, pecans, extract, and salt. Pour into an unbaked pie shell. Bake in a 350 degree oven for 45 minutes, or until firm but not hard.

Serves: 8 people

The Little Playhouse

Growing up, Miss Geraldine remembers playing outside and digging clay out of the creek bank with her fingers. She molded the clay into a tea set and what she called "not-really animals". Once they hardened in the sun, she would play with her handmade toys quite happily for hours.

Miss Geraldine's daddy built a playhouse for her and her sister, Miss Bobbie Ruth. It was a miniature house with running water, a sink and furniture. The windows opened and it had a little pitched roof, just like a real house.

If the girls argued, as sisters sometimes do, Geraldine knew she could win the argument by scaring her sister with a granddaddy long legs spider. She would chase Bobbie Ruth all over and throw the spider on her, making her scream.

Miss Geraldine says with some slight sisterly satisfaction, "I must have done a good job, because she is still afraid of them to this day!"

In later years, the playhouse was used as Miss Daisy's and Uncle Jamie's sleeping quarters even though it was still called the playhouse.

The playhouse, actually was a real house, just built very small.

81

Sweet Potato Pie

This recipe is from my mother Miss Geraldine. She loves to use red jewel sweet potatoes in this pie. She buys them at a roadside stand on her way home from Myrtle Beach, SC. The local farmer grows them in the field behind his produce shed.

4 small sweet potatoes, baked and cooled
½ cup (1 stick) unsalted butter, melted
1 cup sugar
1 teaspoon vanilla extract
One 9-inch pie crust, baked

Preheat the oven to 350 degrees.

Peel the potatoes. Put them in the bowl of an electric stand mixer fitted with whisk. Add the melted butter and sugar. Mix until smooth. Add the vanilla extract. Mix well. Pour the potato mixture into a baked pie crust and bake for 35 minutes. Brush the top with butter when the pie comes out of the oven.

Serves: 8-10 people

Anderson Cooper was so nice! I enjoyed appearing as a guest on *Anderson*, his daytime talk show. On his right is Shane from Talbot Tea.

Apple Pie in a Black Frying Pan

In my family, we never called a cast iron skillet a cast iron skillet. It was always called a black frying pan. My mother, Miss Geraldine, still has her grandmother's black frying pans and uses them regularly.

PIE DOUGH

1 ½ cups unbleached all-purpose flour
2 tablespoons sugar
1 teaspoon salt
½ cup (1 stick) unsalted butter, cold
¼ - ½ cup ice water

Preheat the oven to 350 degrees.

In a food processor, pulse together the flour, sugar, salt, and butter until the mixture is coarse like cornmeal. Add ¼ cup ice water to blend. Add the remaining water a tablespoon at a time until the dough comes together into a ball. Lightly flour the work surface. Knead the dough a few times and flatten into a disk. Wrap and chill until filling is ready.

TOPPING

¼ cup (½ stick) unsalted butter, at room temperature
¼ cup dark brown sugar, firmly packed
2 cups pecans, coarsely chopped

In a bowl, blend the butter and sugar together. Mix in the pecans. Chill.

FILLING

6 apples (Fuji or Gala), peeled and sliced
½ cup light brown sugar, firmly packed
¼ cup granulated sugar
2 tablespoons unbleached all-purpose flour
Juice of 1 fresh lemon
½ - ¾ teaspoon cinnamon

FOR CRUST AFTER 1 HOUR IN THE OVEN

2 tablespoons whole milk
1 tablespoon granulated sugar

Peel and core the apples. Cut the apples into slices about ½-inch thick. Toss them with lemon juice and the remaining ingredients to coat.

Flour your work surface and roll out the chilled dough to ⅛-inch thickness. Put the dough into a 7-or 8-inch greased cast iron skillet or a 9-inch glass pie plate with deep sides. Let the dough hang over the sides. Spoon the filling into the skillet or pie plate. Fold the overhanging dough up over the top of the apples, leaving the center uncovered. Bake 1 hour. Remove from the oven.

Brush the crust with the 2 tablespoons of milk and sprinkle with 1 tablespoon sugar. Crumble the pecan topping over the center of the pie, not on the sugared crust. Return the pie to the oven for 30 minutes, or until the crust is golden and the filling is bubbly. Cool on a rack. Serve warm.

Serves: 8-10 people

Butterscotch Pie

Do you remember the individually wrapped peppermint and butterscotch candies? There was always a candy jar full of them at my grandmothers. That buttery smoothness of the butterscotch in its pretty yellow wrapping was my favorite. This butterscotch pie reminds me of that sweet buttery goodness. Oh, and make lots of peaks on your meringue so you can sneak a peak or two.

¼ cup all-purpose flour
1 cup light brown sugar
1 cup + 2 tablespoons whole milk
3 eggs separated, use whites for meringue
½ stick unsalted butter
Pinch of salt
1 teaspoon vanilla extract
1 cup toasted pecans, optional
One 9-inch pie crust, baked

Preheat the oven to 400 degrees.
Whisk together the flour and sugar on top of a double boiler. Add the milk and egg yolks. Mix well. Add the butter and pinch of salt. Cook until thick. Add the vanilla and pour into the baked pie shell. If you are adding pecans, sprinkle them over the filling now. Top with meringue and bake until the meringue is golden brown.

FOR MERINGUE
Beat the egg whites until soft peaks form. Add 1 or 2 tablespoons of sugar. Continue beating on the highest speed until stiff.
Serves: 8 people

Lemon Pie

Chances are most of us have had a lemon pie made with sweet and delicious condensed milk. This recipe is so simple. The ingredients are probably right there in your kitchen.

3 eggs
1 cup sugar
Pinch of salt
1 lemon zest rind (zest) and juice
2 tablespoons unsalted butter, melted
9-inch pie crust, unbaked

Preheat the oven to 300 degrees.

Beat the eggs. Add the sugar and beat well. Add the salt, juice, zest, and butter. Mix well. Pour the batter into an uncooked pastry shell. Bake 1 hour. Cool completely before topping with whipped cream.

WHIPPED CREAM
1 (8-ounce) carton heavy whipping cream
2 tablespoons powdered sugar

Freeze the mixing bowl and whisk beater 15-20 minutes before making the whipped cream.

Remove the mixing bowl and whisk from the freezer. Pour the heavy whipping cream and 2 tablespoons of powdered sugar into the bowl.

Beat on high until stiff. Do not over beat or the whipping cream will become too loose. Spread on top of the cooled pie.

Serves: 8-10 people

SHARE A SLICE OF LOVE

Yummy

Cheesecakes, Cobblers & Cookies

Anything-But-Plain Cheesecake

For nearly two years, my mother, Miss Geraldine, and I baked cheesecakes for a local restaurant. We know they enjoyed them because they ordered forty cheesecakes every week. The plain cheesecake can be changed to suit your taste by adding broken up pieces of your favorite chocolate, cream-filled cookies, or even your favorite candy bar. The crust can also be made using different types of plain cookies. Don't forget that chocolate sauce poured over a plain cheesecake will make it totally irresistible.

Make sure you use a 10-inch springform pan. These recipes make large cheesecakes. When baking cheesecakes, we always bake them on a cookie sheet lined with foil.

CRUST

3 cups vanilla wafers, (12-ounce box)
1/2 teaspoon cinnamon
2 tablespoons sugar
1/2 cup unsalted butter, melted

Combine all the ingredients in a food processor. Pulse until the wafers are broken into pieces. Continue to process until smooth.

Press the crust into the bottom of a 10-inch springform pan sprayed with non-stick cooking spray.

FILLING

3 (8-ounce) packages cream cheese
1½ cups sugar
4 eggs
2 cups sour cream
1/2 cup heavy whipping cream
2 tablespoons fresh lemon juice
1 tablespoon pure vanilla extract
Pinch of salt

Preheat the oven to 350 degrees.

In the bowl of an electric stand mixer with the paddle fitted, combine the cream cheese and sugar until smooth. Add the eggs. Blend. Scrape down the sides and around the bottom of the bowl and continue to mix until creamy. Add the remaining ingredients. Blend. Scrape the bowl down again. Mix on high for one minute until smooth and fluffy.

Pour the filling onto the crust in a prepared 10-inch springform pan. Bake for 1 hour. Turn off the oven and leave the cheesecake in the oven for 1 hour. DO NOT OPEN THE DOOR!

Remove the cheesecake from the oven and let it cool completely. Remove the springform part of the pan and chill until ready to serve.

Serves: 10-12 people

Peanut Butter Cheesecake

CRUST

1 cup peanuts

2 cups vanilla wafers

¼ cup sugar

½ cup unsalted butter, melted

Put all the ingredients in a food processor. Pulse until the wafers begin to break into pieces. Continue processing until a fine but grainy consistency.

Press the crust into the bottom of a 10-inch springform pan coated with nonstick cooking spray.

FILLING

3 (8-ounce) packages cream cheese

1 jar natural peanut butter, drained (can use liquid in crust)

1 cup granulated sugar

¼ cup light brown sugar

¼ cup unbleached all-purpose flour

Pinch of salt

4 eggs

1 cup heavy whipping cream

1 tablespoon pure vanilla extract

Hint: If your peanut butter has oil on top, you can use it along with the melted butter to make a total of ½ cups for the crust.

Preheat the oven to 350 degrees.

In the mixing bowl of an electric stand mixer, beat the cream cheese until smooth. Add the peanut butter and continue beating until combined. Add the sugars, flour, and salt. Mix well. Add the eggs. Blend. Scrape down the sides and around the bottom of the bowl. Continue beating until smooth.

Add the whipping cream and vanilla. Blend on low speed. Scrape down the sides and around the bottom of the bowl. Continue beating until smooth.

Pour the filling onto the crust in a prepared 10-inch springform pan. Shake the pan back and forth to evenly spread the filling. Bake 1½ hours.

While the cheesecake is baking, prepare the chocolate ganache. Once out of the oven, let the cheesecake cool 15 minutes before pouring the ganache over the top.

GANACHE

2 cups heavy whipping cream

4 cups semisweet chocolate chips

Scald the cream. Remove the cream from heat. Add the chocolate chips. Let the chocolate mixture sit for 10 minutes to melt. Whisk until smooth. Pour the ganache over the top of the cheesecake.

Serves: 10-12 people

95

Pumpkin Cheesecake

This cheesecake is wonderful plain. It is also good with caramel sauce drizzled over it or a dollop of bourbon whipped cream. Don't forget the fresh ground nutmeg!

CRUST
1 bag gingersnap cookies
¼ cup dark brown sugar
½ cup unsalted butter, melted

Put the crust ingredients into the food processor. Pulse until the cookies begin to break into pieces. Continue processing until the mixture is coarse, like cornmeal.

Press the cookie mixture into the bottom of a greased 10-inch springform pan.

FILLING
3 (8-ounce) packages cream cheese
1 (15-ounce) can 100% pure pumpkin
1 cup granulated sugar
¼ cup dark brown sugar
¼ cup unbleached all-purpose flour
Pinch of salt
4 eggs
½ cup heavy whipping cream
1 tablespoon pure vanilla extract

Preheat the oven to 350 degrees.

In the mixing bowl of an electric stand mixer fitted with a paddle, beat the cream cheese until smooth. Add the pumpkin and continue beating until combined. Add the sugars, flour, and salt. Mix well. Add the eggs. Blend. Scrape down the sides and around the bottom of the bowl. Continue beating about 2 minutes, until smooth.

Add the whipping cream and vanilla. Blend on low speed. Scrape down the sides and around the bottom of the bowl. Continue beating about 1 minute, until smooth.

Pour the filing onto the crust in a prepared 10-inch springform pan. Shake the pan back and forth to evenly spread the filling. Bake 1½ hours. Cool completely. Refrigerate overnight for best results before removing the springform side of the pan.

Serves: 10-12 people

Miss Nellie with her great grandson Sam, my youngest son.

Mrs. Tweedy's Chocolate Gravy

When I was ten years old, a new family moved into the house next door. They were Mr. and Mrs. Tweedy and their children Mike, Scott and Lori. They had lived all over the United States because Mr. Tweedy was in the United States Air Force. For a little girl from a small town in the South, this was really exciting. They also drove ninety miles down to Columbia, South Carolina, to buy their groceries at the Fort Jackson Commissary. I always wanted to go with them to this mysterious store, but never got the chance.

On occasion, I did get invited next door to dinner. My favorite was Mrs. Tweedy's specialty, chocolate and biscuits. The biscuits were the soft, flaky, golden brown ones from a can that we simply called canned biscuits. But oh my! That chocolate gravy was something special.

Now, the only thing I had ever seen made in an electric frying pan was either fried chicken or fried pork chops. Mrs. Tweedy had a better use for her pan. She used it to make her wonderful chocolate gravy.

I don't imagine too many people still use an electric frying pan. Luckily, this recipe works just fine in a skillet on the stove. Here is her recipe along with my thanks to her daughter, my friend Lori, for sharing it.

1½ cups granulated sugar
2 tablespoons cocoa
4 tablespoons all-purpose flour
2 cups of water (warm)
1 teaspoon of vanilla
2 tablespoons butter
Pinch of salt (if using unsalted butter)

Mix the sugar, cocoa, and flour in a heavy medium-sized saucepan. (Mix thoroughly to remove any lumps). Place the pan on the burner and add water. Bring to a boil and cook until desired thickness. Add the vanilla and butter. Stir to combine.

Serve over warm buttered biscuits.
Makes enough for 8-12 biscuits.

Hint: Homemade are best, but sacrilegious canned biscuits will work, too!

Blackberry Cobbler

On the days when we went blackberry picking, we always made blackberry jelly and a great big blackberry cobbler that same night. The taste of the blackberry cobbler was worth all the chiggers and scratches we got from the very sharp prickles that are all over the bushes.

DOUGH
2 cups unbleached all-purpose flour
3 tablespoons granulated sugar
1 teaspoon salt
½ cup lard, cold
¼ cup unsalted butter, cold
½ - ¾ cup ice water (water with ice in it)

Preheat the oven to 400 degrees.

In a food processor, combine the flour, sugar, and salt. Pulse slightly. Add the lard and butter. Pulse until the mixture is coarse like cornmeal. Add ¼ cup ice water. Pulse to combine. Add the remaining ice water, 1 tablespoon at a time, until the dough forms into a ball. Turn the dough out onto plastic wrap and knead a few times and form into a disk. Wrap and chill until the blackberry filling is ready.

FILLING
4 cups fresh blackberries
1 tablespoon fresh lemon juice
½ cup water
1 cup granulated sugar
¼ cup light brown sugar
¼ cup unbleached all-purpose flour
2 tablespoons tapioca
Pinch of salt

In a nonreactive mixing bowl, add the berries. Toss with lemon juice and water. In a separate bowl, combine the sugars with the flour, tapioca, and salt. Mix the dry ingredients into the berries. Set aside.

Butter the bottom and sides of a 2-quart cobbler pan, square baking dish, or round dish with sloping sides.

Lightly flour your work surface and roll out ¾ of the chilled dough. Line a 2-quart cobbler pan bottom and sides with dough. Pour in the berries.

Roll out the remaining dough. Cut into strips and lay on top of the berries. You can do a weave if you like. Egg wash (1 egg mixed with 1 teaspoon milk or water) the dough and sprinkle with 1 tablespoon of granulated sugar.

Bake at 400 degrees for 30-40 minutes, or until the crust is golden and the berries are bubbly.

Serves: 10-12 people

Easy Individual Cobblers

This is an easy way to have a nice, fresh fruit cobbler without having to make dough. Individual desserts really make your company feel special.

3 cups fresh berries, (blueberries, blackberries or strawberries)
½ cup granulated sugar, plus 2 tablespoons for sprinkling on fruit
4 tablespoons (½ stick) unsalted butter, at room temperature
1 large egg
1 teaspoon vanilla extract
1 cup unbleached all-purpose flour
½ teaspoon baking soda
¼ teaspoon salt
½ cup whole-fat buttermilk, well shaken

Preheat the oven to 400 degrees.

Butter six 1½ cup ramekins. Put ½ cup fruit into each. If you are using strawberries, slice them first. Sprinkle each ramekin of fruit with 1 teaspoon sugar. Set aside.

In the bowl of an electric stand mixer, cream together the butter and ½ cup sugar for about two minutes, until light and fluffy. Add the egg and vanilla. Blend slightly. Add the flour, baking soda, salt, and buttermilk. Mix at low speed until just incorporated.

Spoon the batter evenly over the fruit. Place the ramekins on parchment paper on a cookie sheet. Bake 30 minutes, or until golden brown. Serve warm.

Serves: 6 people

Danny Youssef, our web marketing guru, Barbara Corcoran and myself outside the Daisy Cakes bakery and headquarters.

Peach Bread Pudding

This bread pudding went to the *CBS Baking Show* casting call in Nashville, TN. I served it with homemade buttermilk ice cream, homemade caramel sauce and salted pecans. This recipe needs to start a day ahead of time and be refrigerated overnight. The tanginess of the buttermilk ice cream wonderfully sets off the bread pudding.

10 mini croissants, a day or two old, broken into 4 pieces each
8 peaches, peeled and diced
1 lemon, juiced
8 eggs
1/2 cup light brown sugar
1/2 cup granulated sugar
A good pinch of salt
1/4 cup (1/2 stick) unsalted butter, melted
1 teaspoon vanilla extract
3 cups heavy whipping cream

Thoroughly butter a 9 x 9-inch baking dish.

Put the broken croissant pieces into the bottom of a buttered 9 x 9-inch baking dish.

Peel and dice the peaches and toss with lemon juice. Set aside.

In a large mixing bowl, beat the eggs.

Add both sugars, salt, and melted butter. Add the vanilla extract and whipping cream. Whisk until smooth and pale yellow in color. Fold in the peaches. Pour the peach mixture on top of the croissant pieces.

Cover and refrigerate overnight.

Preheat the oven to 325 degrees. Bake the bread pudding on a baking sheet to prevent it from bubbling over in your oven.

Bake 1 1/2 hours. The bread pudding should be puffed in the middle as well as on the sides and somewhat firm when shaken. The bread pudding will fall slightly and set while cooling.

Serves: 12 people

Hint: For this dish, I like to use a stone baking dish.

That handsome Nate Berkus! He was such a funny and gracious host when I was featured on his show with Barbara Corcoran.

SHARE A SLICE OF LIFE

Banana or Pineapple Pudding

How many times when you were younger did you literally beg your mother, "Please don't use all the custard in the banana pudding! I want to scrape the pot and lick the spoon!" This custard is so delicious that you'll want to do the same thing! It is just that good! To make the banana or pineapple pudding, all you need is your favorite vanilla wafers along with bananas or pineapple.

You can assemble the banana or pineapple pudding in an 8 x 8-inch glass dish or individual bowls. Just layer the wafers, bananas, and pudding until your dish is filled. It's delicious. I highly recommend doubling the recipe.

PLAIN CUSTARD

    ¾ cup sugar
    1 tablespoon self rising flour
    1 large can evaporated milk
    2 eggs
    1 teaspoon vanilla extract

In a medium saucepan, whisk together the sugar and flour. Add the milk and eggs. Whisk thoroughly until smooth. Cook over medium heat until thick, stirring constantly. Remove from heat. Add the vanilla. Cover with plastic wrap touching the pudding to prevent a thick, rubbery film from forming on the custard. Refrigerate until cool.

Makes 2 cups of custard.

BANANA OR PINEAPPLE PUDDING

custard
1 box vanilla wafers
1 (20-ounce) can crushed pineapple, drained or 4 large bananas, sliced

To make the banana or pineapple pudding, let the custard cool just a little before assembling.

Line bottom of dish with vanilla wafers. Spoon drained pineapple or sliced bananas over vanilla wafers. Spread ½ of custard over the top of pineapple or bananas. Add another layer of vanilla wafers, then pineapple or bananas and custard. Stand vanilla wafers up around top of dish and finish off with a layer of wafers. Let cool at room temperature.

Serves: 10-12 people

Snicker Doodles

This recipe is reprinted from the very first cookbook I ever owned, *The Cookie Book* by Eva Moore (USA: Scholastic Book Services with The Seabury Press, Inc., 1973) pages 50-51.

½ cup (1 stick) unsalted butter
¾ cup sugar
1 egg
1¼ cups flour
¼ teaspoon salt
½ teaspoon baking soda
1 teaspoon cream of tartar
1 tablespoon sugar
1 tablespoon cinnamon

MAKE THE COOKIE DOUGH

Get a large mixing bowl. Measure the butter and put it in the bowl. Measure the sugar and add it. Cream the butter and the sugar together.

Get a cup, and break the egg into it. Pour the egg into the creamed mixture. Beat it all together. Beat it and beat it. Set the mixing bowl aside.

Measure the flour, the salt, the baking soda, and the cream of tartar into a sifter. Sift them into a bowl.

Dump half the sifted ingredients into the egg mixture. Stir with a mixing spoon. Stir slowly; stir hard. Then add the rest of the sifted ingredients and stir some more. You will have a sticky light-yellow batter.

Cover the mixing bowl with a plate and put it in the refrigerator. Leave it there for one hour. The dough will get cold and hard.

GET READY TO SHAPE THE COOKIES

Just before you are ready to take the dough out of the refrigerator, let the oven get hot. Set it at 400 degrees.

Mix the sugar and cinnamon on a small plate.

When the hour is up, take the cookie dough out of the refrigerator. Get a cookie sheet or two. (You do not have to grease them.) You are ready to make the cookies.

SHAPE AND BAKE THE COOKIES

Be sure your hands are clean. Break off a bit of cold dough, about the size of a walnut, and roll it into a ball.

Then roll the ball around in the dish of cinnamon-sugar. Put it on the cookie sheet. Make more balls the same way. Leave a lot of room around each one on the cookie sheet.

When the cookie sheet is full, put it into the oven—slowly and carefully. Don't let the balls roll together. (If you have another cookie sheet, get another batch ready while the first batch is baking.)

Don't open the oven door for at least 10 minutes. Then look—magic! The cinnamon-sugar balls have become flat and crinkly snicker doodles! Are they brown at the bottom edges? Then they are done. If the edges are still not brown, let them bake for two minutes more.

These cookies are soft when you take them off the cookie sheet. Lift them up carefully with a spatula and set them on a wire rack to cool.

Makes 24 crisp cookies.

How It All Started

Our backyard neighbors were Joann and Earl Seay and their children Randy, Sandon, Shalon, and Stacy. Mama and Miss Joann were the best of friends. They would borrow eggs, milk, sugar, and other things they were out of, over the backyard fence.

Many times I climbed over that fence to get to Miss Joann's kitchen. More than once, I got my clothes caught on the spikes at the top and had to scream for help to get unstuck. I would get in trouble and not climb for a while. For some reason that fence always called out to me. Besides, it was quicker than going around through the woods.

I still have the cookbook Miss Joann gave me. I believe it's the first cookbook I ever baked from while in the fifth grade.

Fun to Make · Easy to Bake

THE COOKIE BOOK

by Eva Moore   Illustrations by Tālivaldis Stub

Gingerbread Man Cookies

Each year for Ballet Spartanburg's production of *The Nutcracker*, I bake 450 of these gingerbread cookies to be sold over the performance weekend. Rolling dough is like relaxation therapy to me.

I became involved with Ballet Spartanburg when my daughter Shelby took ballet classes for fifteen years. She went on to the University at St. Andrews in Scotland. Fortunately, my family still has the privilege of being a small part of the ballet for this very special event.

Thank you, Trish McCallister, for sharing your recipe.

¹/₃ cup shortening
1 cup light or dark brown sugar
1¹/₂ cups molasses
²/₃ cup ice water

In large bowl of an electric stand mixer, using the paddle, combine the first three ingredients. Add the ice water.

SIFT TOGETHER
7 cups unbleached all-purpose flour
2 teaspoons baking soda
1 teaspoon salt
1 teaspoon allspice
1 teaspoon ginger
1 teaspoon ground cloves
1 teaspoon cinnamon

Mix the flour mixture into the shortening and water mixture.

Roll the dough to ³/₈-inch thickness and cut.

FOR THE COOKIES
Bake at 350 degrees for 12-15 minutes.

FOR THE ORNAMENTS
Bake at 250 degrees for 1 hour. BEFORE BAKING—use a regular drinking straw to make a hole in the top of the cookie to put your ribbon through.

If the amount of this recipe is too much for your mixer to hold, cut it in half.

Makes forty 3-inch cookies or ornaments.

Sauces

Strawberry Fields Forever Filling

It was always great fun to go strawberry picking with my grandmother, Miss Nervielee, even if it was a long drive to her favorite strawberry patch. Rows of strawberries ran as far as the eye could see. We grabbed our gallon buckets and started picking. Our buckets were full in no time. I loved to pretend mine was a treasure chest full of red rubies. On the way out of the strawberry patch, there was always the last and most perfect strawberry that had to fit on top of the already over-flowing mound of gleaming red jewels.

When we got back to the house, the berries were rinsed, sliced and cooked into batches of strawberry jam and this wonderful strawberry filling. We probably ate as many as we cooked.

STRAWBERRY FILLING
2 cups sugar
Pinch of salt
¼ cup cornstarch
1½ cups sliced, fresh strawberries
¾ cup water

In a medium saucepan, blend together the sugar, salt, and cornstarch. Add the strawberries and water. Cover and cook over low heat about 15 minutes, or until thick.
Makes 2 pints.

Hint: You can use different fruit for this recipe. Blackberries, blueberries, and pineapple also work well. Because each fruit has different levels of sweetness, adjust the amount of sugar accordingly. This filling will keep in the refrigerator for up to a week. It also freezes nicely.

For the Grown-Ups
For a grown-up sauce, add a tablespoon or two of bourbon or dark rum.

Chocolate Sauce

A delicious sauce to pour over plain cheesecake or on top of ice cream.

1 cup sugar
¼ cup cocoa
½ cup half & half or whipping cream
Pinch of salt
4 tablespoons (½ stick) unsalted butter
½ teaspoon vanilla extract

Combine all the ingredients in a medium-sized saucepan. Cook over medium heat until the sugar is dissolved. Remove from heat. Add the vanilla.

This chocolate sauce will keep in the refrigerator for up to a week.

Makes 1 pint.

Caramel Sauce

Drizzle this sauce over pumpkin cheesecake or pecan pie. It can also be used on apple pie or on top of ice cream.

1 cup light brown sugar
1 cup granulated sugar
4 tablespoons (½ stick) unsalted butter
2 tablespoons cornstarch
2 cups heavy whipping cream
Pinch of salt
2 teaspoons vanilla extract

Combine the light brown sugar, granulated sugar, butter, cornstarch, whipping cream, and salt in a heavy medium-sized saucepan. Bring to boil, whisking constantly. Reduce to medium heat and continue whisking until thickened. Remove from heat and stir in the vanilla. Put in a glass container and keep in the refrigerator. Keeps up to 1 month.

Makes 2 pints.

Here I am with my mother, Miss Geraldine, Whitney Chen and Jeff Mauro of Season 7 of Food Network Star.

Behind the Cupboard with Daisy Cakes

Producing our cookbook, just like our cakes, is a BIG team effort! We want to acknowledge our food styling and photography team: Photographer Lynne Harty, Food Stylist Beth Buzogany and Photo Stylist Chris Bryant.

Above: Beth Buzogany art directs the powdered sugar! Styling the food takes a lot of patience and finesse. Top right: Chris Bryant talks about the photo setup with Beth. Bottom right: Beth puts the finishing touches on a 2 page spread setup, for Photographer Lynne Harty—who is not in front of the camera where we can see her!

Above and left: Beth and Chris stage the photo setup for the 2 page tea party spread. The fabulous garden was such a charming setting. When we talked over the look and feel of our book, we wanted it to be friendly, inviting and authentically Southern. I think the team did a great job conveying my feelings about our food. What do you think?

Right: Happy Baking! Thanks for sharing our dream! Now go out there and Share a Slice of Love!
Front, left to right: Photographer Lynne Harty, Daisy Cakes CEO Kim Daisy. Back, left to right: Food Stylist Beth Buzogany and Photo Stylist Chris Bryant.

My Heirloom Recipes

My Heirloom Recipes

My Heirloom Recipes

My Heirloom Recipes

My Heirloom Recipes

My Heirloom Recipes

My Heirloom Recipes

My Heirloom Recipes

Kitchen Equipment Notes & Tips

Stand Mixer

The recipes in this book call for a stand mixer. It is my favorite piece of kitchen equipment. It is expensive but will last a lifetime. However, you do not have to use a stand mixer for any of the recipes in this book. A hand mixer will do the job.

Tube Pan

This is a pan with a tube in the center. May or may not have a false removable bottom.

Angel Food Cake Pan

This is a tube cake pan whose bottom and tube are removable. The new pans have 'feet' that stick out of the top of the pan. When inverted, the cake can cool completely in the pan without touching the surface of the counter. Older angel food cake pans may not have the feet, but you can turn the cake pan upside down on a narrow necked bottle to cool.

Spring Form Pan

This is a pan used mainly for cheesecakes. The sides have a spring attachment that allows them to be removed after baking. They can also be used for other baked goods besides cheesecake.

Bundt Pan

This is a heavy cake pan that sometimes has designs in the body of the pan that give a lovely look to the finished cake. Bundt cakes are usually not frosted but drizzled with a glaze following baking.

Round Cake pan

These come in many different sizes. I recommend having two 8-inch and three 9-inch pans in your kitchen.

Rectangular Cake Pan

This is usually 9 inches x 13 inches and is used for a sheet cake. Can be metal or glass.

Loaf Pans

These are rectangular deep pans usually used for breads or cake like breads. Three small pans equals one regular size pan.

Black Frying Pan (Cast Iron Skillet)

This is made of iron and is something every cook should have. It gives superior heat retention and even baking. Cornbread is perfect baked in a cast iron skillet. The older models require seasoning with oil and baking at low temperatures before use, but today you can purchase a preseasoned skillet online. In this book a cast iron skillet is called a black frying pan.

Pie Pan	Pie pans come in metal, glass and ceramic. The size and type perform the same, so choose your favorite. Pie pans have sloping sides.
Tart Pans	Tart pans have removable bottoms and straight sides. They come in a variety of shapes and sizes.
Pie Weights	Pie weights are used to put in the crust when you blind bake, or prebake the crust. You put foil in the crust and add the weights for the first 15 minutes and then remove them to finish baking off the crust. Dry beans work just as well as weights and can be saved in a plastic bag to be used over and over.
Biscuit Cutter	Biscuit cutters are sharp and cut precisely; this helps the biscuit rise when baked. You can use a glass but it will push the layers of the dough down and the result won't be as good as if you used a cutter.
Ramekin	A small dish for baking and serving an individual portion of food. Usually used for custards or cobblers.
Skewer	You can purchase a cake tester or you may use a toothpick to test the doneness of a cake. My grandmother would sometimes pull a piece of straw from a broom to test the cake and it worked just fine.
Oven Thermometer	This is a useful item to check the temperature of your oven. Certain recipes must have very accurate temperatures to work. It is inexpensive and readily available. Most grocery stores carry them.
Nonreactive Pan	A pan that does not react with the food in it. Can be stainless steel, glass, enameled or ceramic.

Daisy Cakes' Family Tree

Miss Nervielee

Miss Nellie

Miss Daisy

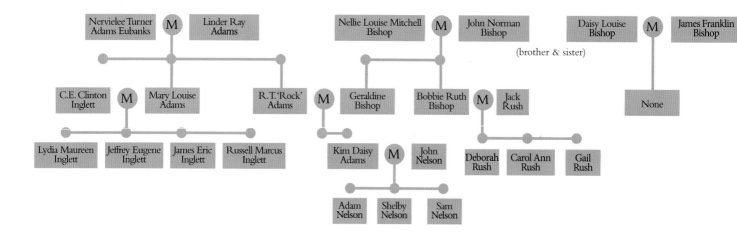

Nervielee Turner Adams Eubanks **M** Linder Ray Adams

Nellie Louise Mitchell Bishop **M** John Norman Bishop

Daisy Louise Bishop **M** James Franklin Bishop

(brother & sister)

C.E. Clinton Inglett **M** Mary Louise Adams — R.T. 'Rock' Adams

Geraldine Bishop — Bobbie Ruth Bishop **M** Jack Rush

None

Lydia Maureen Inglett — Jeffrey Eugene Inglett — James Eric Inglett — Russell Marcus Inglett

Kim Daisy Adams **M** John Nelson

Deborah Rush — Carol Ann Rush — Gail Rush

Adam Nelson — Shelby Nelson — Sam Nelson